Separate Lives

Separate Lives

Why Siblings Are So Different

JUDY DUNN and ROBERT PLOMIN

BasicBooks

A Division of HarperCollins*Publishers*

Library of Congress Cataloging-in-Publication Data
Dunn, Judy, 1939–
    Separate lives: why siblings are so different / Judy Dunn,
Robert Plomin.
        p.   cm.
    Includes bibliographical references and index.
    ISBN 0–465–07688–2 (cloth)
    ISBN 0–465–07689–0 (paper)
    1. Brothers and sisters.   2. Individual differences.   3. Nature
and nurture.   I. Plomin, Robert, 1948–   II. Title.
BF723.S43D85   1990   90-80254
155.44′3—dc20   .   CIP

To those with very different lives
within our families:
Sophie, William, and Paul;
Benjamin and Joseph.

Contents

Prologue   ix

1   A Challenge   1

2   Differences in Nature   21

3   Differences in Nurture   40

4   The Impact of Parents   60

5   Sibling Influences   88

6   Beyond the Family   115

7   Chance   135

8   Implications   151

Notes   173

References   191

Index   205

Prologue

The first thing she noticed was the boots, surprising in the formality of the conference room in the prestigious CIBA building in Portland Place, just by Regents Park in London. It was October 1981, an international CIBA conference on the development of temperament. Among the other conference participants ranged around the comfortable room, he lounged back casually with the boots stretched out for all to see. She wondered who the young man was—probably another arrogant American come to "tell it like it is" to us "poor Brits."

She was much more interested in this conference than in most of the international jet-set conferences lampooned so well by David Lodge in his novels on academia. The topic—temperament—had drawn developmental psychologists, clinicians, and a new species, behavioral geneticists, all with a common interest in early appearing personality traits thought by many to be genetically based. Developmental psychologists were beginning to notice how different one infant is from the next, not just in mental abilities and language ability, but also in personality. Clinicians were still shaking off the constraints of the view that all the bad aspects of personality could be attributed to poor mothering, a "mal de mère" syndrome. Behavioral geneticists—the few practitioners in this new field—were beginning to provide an empirical base for the idea that infants are different genetically, not just environmentally; the idea that heredity affects behavioral development, especially behavior as complex as personality, which is the core of who we are, was still considered naughty—not to be contemplated seriously—but not nasty, as it had been during the 1970s.

Behavioral genetics began only a few streets away from the CIBA building. Here in London, over a century ago, Sir Francis Galton, cousin to Charles Darwin, was so taken with the *Origin of Species* that, after a productive career as an inventor and explorer, he took up the problem of human heredity. He pioneered the use of family, twin, and adoption methods to disentangle the genetic and environmental threads interwoven in the fabric of human development. On the basis of his large-scale family pedigree studies, he concluded that "nature prevails enormously over nurture." Although Darwin was much more interested in differences between species than in differences between individuals within the human species, he was persuaded by Galton's work: "I am inclined to agree with Francis Galton in believing that education and environment produce only a small effect on the mind of any one, and that most of our qualities are innate."

Systematic twin and adoption studies began in earnest in the 1920s, at a time when the influence of heredity was accepted in the behavioral sciences. The next decade brought the horrors of the Nazi regime with its pseudogenetic theories about racial differences as a rationale for the slaughter of Jews, Gypsies, and others; revulsion toward the Nazis combined with influential research by psychologists on the principles of learning effectively eliminated research on heredity and human development. After the Second World War, psychology was dominated by the view that nurture alone, rather than nature, is responsible for behavioral differences among children.

By the 1960s, a more balanced view that recognized the importance of nature as well as nurture was beginning to re-emerge, but it was stamped out in the violent reaction against a 1969 article by Arthur Jensen which suggested that racial differences in IQ scores may be genetic in origin. The etiology of average group differences such as those between racial groups or social classes is still not understood, in part because the origins of average group differences are so difficult to study. Nonetheless, the early 1980s saw a dramatic shift toward an acceptance of the existence of genetic influence on individual differences in behaviors such as mental abilities, mental illness, and personality. The wave of acceptance of genetic influence that began to build in the 1960s but was held back in the 1970s crashed into the 1980s.

In 1981, in that comfortable CIBA conference room, the conference participants were discussing temperament. She herself studied siblings, an interest that had grown from personal experience with her three very different children. She was just finishing a book on siblings' social and personality development. It is impossible to study siblings and not to think about heredity. Indeed, Solomon Diamond, in an early book on temperament in 1957, made the interesting observation that psychologists tend to be environmentalists until they have more than one child. With the first one, it is easy to rationalize everything environmentally. "She's shy because we didn't take her out very much as a baby." (Or just as often, "She's shy because we took her out too much as a baby.") But when a second child proves very different from the first, it is much more difficult to come up with environmental explanations— "We didn't treat them *that* differently."

PROLOGUE

From her research as well as observation of her own three children, who included a pair of twins, she believed that heredity could explain some differences between siblings growing up in the same family. But she was sure that sibling differences were not all to be explained by genetics—siblings are too different for that. They are first-degree relatives and thus share half their genes, which means that if a trait were entirely genetic siblings should be 50 percent similar as well as 50 percent different. But siblings are much less than 50 percent similar. The differences between them must surely reflect differences in their experiences as well as differences in heredity. But what were the key experiences that led to brothers and sisters being so different? Her work was beginning to suggest both that parents treat their children quite differently and that siblings differ in how they behave toward each other.

She was roused from her musings by the arrival of the next speaker at the podium. To her surprise, the speaker, whom she had assumed would be an "elder statesman," because he had published a book on temperament and was one of the leaders in the field of behavioral genetics was the young American man wearing cowboy boots. She had been concerned that her own talk was to follow a presentation on behavioral genetics: her talk would clash with what would surely be his message—that everything's genetic. Her fears grew as he quickly presented twin and adoption data that built a strong case for the importance of genetic influence in personality. But then he said, "What I'm going to talk about today is something else."

He went on to say that for the past decade it had been important to get the message across that heredity has an appreciable effect on human development, even for traits as complex as personality. However, the lurching from antipathy toward acceptance of genetic influence was in danger of swinging the pendulum of fashion too far—from environmentalism to biological determinism. A second message from these same behavioral genetic data was important: It's not all genetic. Identical twins are 100 percent similar genetically. Yet they are only about 50 percent similar in personality, and most of this similarity is due to genetic factors. Why, then, are they so different? Up until now, he said, the surprise had been that identical twins are so similar, which suggests genetic influence. Since twins are identical genetically, it has to be environmental influence that makes the twins different from one another. Yet how can they be so different when they grow up together in the same family environment? Or do they? He ended his talk by saying that the important question now was to understand why siblings growing up in the same family are so different.

Speakers at conferences frequently thank the previous speaker, often in a condescending manner as a form of one-upmanship. On this occasion, her appreciation was genuine and almost too fulsome, as recorded in the unexpurgated conference proceedings published as a book in 1982. After the morning session, the two were seated together at a sumptuous CIBA luncheon and began talking excitedly about the implications for researchers, clinicians, and parents of combining their two approaches—his, the large-scale study of adopted versus biological siblings and identical versus fraternal twins, and hers, the detailed examination of what happens between different family members—to the study of separate lives within the family.

This book is the result.

1

A Challenge

My mother had a good deal of trouble with me but I think she enjoyed it. She had none at all with my brother Henry, who was two years younger than I, and I think that the unbroken monotony of his goodness and truthfulness and obedience would have been a burden to her but for the relief and variety which I furnished in the other direction. . . . I never knew Henry to do a vicious thing toward me or toward anyone else—but he frequently did righteous ones that cost me as heavily. It was his duty to report me, when I needed reporting and neglected to do it myself, and he was very faithful in discharging that duty. He is Sid in Tom Sawyer. *But Sid was not Henry. Henry was a very much finer and better boy than ever Sid was.*

—Mark Twain, *Autobiography*

Mark Twain, writing of his brother and himself, leaves us in no doubt about the differences between the two of them. The famous incidents of Tom Sawyer's troubles with Sid are drawn straight from their life together as children. While Henry was, as Twain puts it, "the best boy in the whole region . . . exasperatingly good . . ." it is clear that Twain himself was far from good. "I took it out of Henry. . . . I often took it out of him—sometimes as an advance payment for something which I hadn't yet done."

Consider another pair of brothers, born a few years later into a very different world from the "almost invisible village" in Missouri where Mark Twain and his brother were growing up—William James, who founded American psychology, and Henry James, the novelist. The striking differences between these two, and indeed all five James siblings, are commented on by all who write about them: their parents, their friends, their biographers, and the siblings themselves. Henry, writing of the four James brothers and their sister Alice in *A Small Boy and Others*, comments, "We were, to my sense . . . such a company of characters and such a picture of differences, and withal so fused and united and interlocked, that each of us . . . pleads for preservation." As his biographer Leon Edel notes, Henry characterizes himself as unadaptive, aloof, lacking William's easy gregariousness and savoir faire, envying William's effortless talents and capabilities. William, too, jokingly complains of Henry's unsociability in a letter to his parents: "Never did I see a so-much uninterested creature in the affairs of those about him. He is a good soul, though, in his way too. . . ." The differences in personality between William and Henry were indeed notable: William active, energetic, effervescent, with a vibrant personality; Henry much quieter, less confident or secure.

It is rare for siblings to attain such prominence in different fields as the James brothers. Who has heard of the siblings of Cervantes, Descartes, or Rembrandt? Occasionally siblings become known for their collaborative work, such as Jacques and Jean Bernoulli, who developed calculus, and Orville and Wilbur Wright, who developed the airplane; or for common creative interests, as with the sons of Johann Sebastian Bach—Carl Philipp Emanuel, Wilhelm Friedemann, and Johann Christian. But even when siblings share a creative field, their personalities and the nature of their achievements can be strikingly different. The poet Alfred Housman and his brother Laurence grew up together in a conventional High Tory family in England; both became writers, but there were few other similarities between them, as children or as adults. According to Henry Maas, the editor of Alfred's letters,

> Alfred resembled Laurence only in the ability to write. Otherwise he was a complete contrast. Where Laurence was diffuse, impulsive and warm-hearted, Alfred was precise, disciplined and reserved. Laurence lavished his gifts on too many books, Alfred constricted his poems within the bounds of a tiny *oeuvre*. Laurence was always getting into trouble, Alfred carefully kept out of it. Laurence was a visionary and idealist, to whom his elder brother must at times have seemed a reactionary pedant.

It is with such differences between siblings that the argument of our book begins. Our study will take us well beyond the contemplation of a few striking individuals, and even beyond the relationships between siblings, to consider the origins and development of differences between people. It will bring us to a new perspective on how families influence those differences, a perspective with important implications for parents, clinicians, and researchers. For parents, the differences between their children can be a source of delight or exasperation, and the origins of these differences a major concern; for adults reflecting on their abilities and personalities, it is surely a matter of puzzling intrigue why they should be so different from their brothers or sisters.

The first thread in our argument is that these differences between siblings, especially provocative and intriguing in the case of such remarkable individuals as the James brothers, are *not* in themselves exceptional or extraordinary—not solely the unusual divergence of outstanding and especially gifted individuals. Quite to the contrary: all research that includes information on more than one child within a family tells the same story, that siblings generally differ markedly from one another.

This book is based on evidence from systematic research, but we also draw for illustration from the evidence of a number of writers, their families, and their biographers as we examine the question of why children growing up in the same family are so different. The justifications for considering these writers are several. They themselves frequently wrote with particular insight and sensitivity about their childhood experiences. In their portrayal of the intensities and influences of their childhood world—in both autobiographical and fictional writing—they illuminate the power and the significance of particular relationships and experiences. In addition, for these illustrious people we frequently have access not only to their own accounts of their childhood experiences and family relationships, but also to the letters they wrote and received; to the views and perspectives of other participants in their family world, including their siblings' descriptions of their shared and separate experiences; and to the interpretations offered by biographers. The accounts of perceptive writers and their families about their childhood worlds are of special importance. "Nobody, who has not been in the interior of a family, can say what the difficulties of any individual of that family may be" was the comment of Jane Austen's Emma to Mr. Knightley in *Emma*, and it is a chastening one for psychologists attempting to understand the patterns of family influence.

We start, then, with the *differences* between several writers and their brothers and sisters. Note that our subjects come from a range of social and historical worlds: from eighteenth-century England and France, rural nineteenth-century America, working-class Ireland and England; from conventional well-to-do upper-middle-class families, eccentric aristocratic families, highly cultured literary families, and families growing up in poverty and stress. In all the families, striking differences between the siblings growing up together are evident from every source. Indeed, it is rare to find a writer whose biographer fails to stress the differences between the subject and his or her siblings.

Thus the poet John Keats, whose intense early relationship with his two surviving brothers ("passing the love of women" as he himself commented) and his younger sister Fanny continued throughout his life, was already in early childhood markedly different from them. He had a tempestuous personality, and was described as "violent and ungovernable" as a 5-year-old; as playful and with an extraordinary vivacity; as subject to extreme melancholy, with a "horrid morbidity of living"—all in striking contrast to his siblings (toward whom he was exceptionally kind and responsible), especially his "sweetly behaved" ("stodgy" in the terms of his biographer Robert Gittings) younger sister.

An equally notable contrast is seen in the personalities of the siblings in the family of Keats's contemporary, Percy Bysshe Shelley. Shelley himself was exuberant, mischievous, domineering, and daring, his four sisters adoring and compliant followers. His sister Elizabeth was his closest companion in his wild escapades, the other three being frequently frightened by his games and experiments. Hellen, the third sister, wrote about her feelings about taking part in his terrifying experiments:

> When my brother commenced his studies in chemistry, and practiced electricity upon us, I confess my pleasure in it was

5

entirely negatived by terror at its effects. Whenever he came to me with his piece of folded brown packing-paper under his arm and a bit of wire and a bottle . . . my heart would sink with fear at his approach; but shame kept me silent, and, with as many others as he could collect, we were placed hand-in-hand around the nursery table to be electrified.

Among the great writers of the nineteenth and early twentieth centuries, examples of sibling differences abound. The Brontës are a famous example: Branwell passionate, violent, uncontrolled; Maria, who was the model for Helen Burns in *Jane Eyre*, mildness, fortitude, wisdom, and patience personified; Charlotte desperately vulnerable to pain and shyness. The Proust brothers, too, differed notably, as described by George Painter in his masterly biography, with Marcel the son who arouses anxiety and admiration and Robert the solid figure who pleases and obeys. Leo Tolstoy was apparently far more emotionally intense than his brothers Nicholas, Sergey, and Dmitry—nicknamed by them "Lyova Ryova," or "Leo Crybaby." A tutor passed this judgment on their scholastic differences: "Nicholas is both willing and able; Sergey is able but not willing; Dmitry is willing but not able; and Leo is neither."

Such differences are often portrayed vividly by the writers themselves. Tom Sawyer and Sid are by no means the only brothers whose differences are amusingly or ironically highlighted for us. Some siblings denounced each other: Thomas Mann's *Reflections of a Non-Political Man* is described by his biographer Nigel Hamilton as "an assault on all the ideas and postures he identified with Heinrich . . . a vitriolic and mean denunciation of his own brother."

In contrast, it is evident that for some siblings the differences between them in personality in no way detracted from their intellectual sympathy or support for one another—Mark Twain and his brother, for example, or the Brontë sisters. We are not concerned here with the quality of the relationships between the siblings, nor the role that tensions generated by sibling differences may have played in the literary and intellectual creativity of these writers—matters on which literary biographers have speculated at length. We wish to emphasize a single, simple point: that particular persons growing up in the same family differed very much from one another in personality, talents, emotional security, confidence, and style. These differences set the stage for our argument on the development of individual differences between people in general.

The catalogue of notable differences is as long as the list of writers we choose to consider. George Eliot, D. H. Lawrence, Virginia Woolf, Katherine Mansfield, Rudyard Kipling, Oscar Wilde, Charles Dodgson (Lewis Carroll) all differed very much from their brothers and sisters, as indicated in their fictional writing, their family letters, and the information amassed by their biographers. And yet, a critic might argue, examples could just as easily have been found to document similarities between brothers and sisters. Furthermore, since these biographies concern exceptionally talented and imaginative people, perhaps any differences between them and their siblings are unusual, even exaggerated by their biographers. In other words, how representative are these examples?

There are of course similarities as well as differences between siblings evident in the writers' biographical and autobiographical material. The Brontë siblings shared extraordinary imaginative gifts and literary talents. From childhood, Virginia Woolf and her sister Vanessa both showed exceptional sensibilities, imagination, and creativity.

In our biographical examples we emphasize differences rather than similarities for several reasons. First, the surprise is that children growing up in the same family are so different (a point amply documented in the biographical and autobiographical material listed in the notes for this chapter); their similarities are less surprising. Second—and this will be the point of the next chapter—what runs in families producing similarities is DNA, not family environment. That is, what little resemblance there is among siblings is due to hereditary similarity, not to the experience of growing up in the same family. Sibling differences, on the other hand, emerge for reasons of nurture as well as nature.

Finally, and most important, our examples from writers and their siblings illustrate the point that stands out from the mountains of empirical evidence collected about siblings in systematic studies. These data, as we will see in the overview that follows, show that sibling differences greatly exceed similarities for most characteristics. Our interest lies with psychological characteristics such as cognitive abilities, personality, and mental illness, in part because behavioral traits seem especially likely to be affected by life within the family. However, we begin with a review of physical traits and disease because they provide a backdrop against which psychological traits can be contrasted.

PHYSICAL TRAITS AND DISEASE

Over a hundred years ago, Francis Galton conducted the first systematic studies of family resemblance, initially using height and other physical characteristics. In a sample of nearly 1,000 males reported in 1889, he found that adult brothers on average differ by about 1.5 inches in height. A great deal of variability surrounds this average. For example, 15 percent of the brothers differed by less than half an inch; a few differed by as much as a foot. For weight, Galton's data showed an approximately 20-pound difference on average for same-sex siblings.

Although physical differences between siblings are large, interpreting the extent of sibling differences requires that we compare their differences to differences in the rest of the population. That is, we need to know how big the average sibling height difference of 1.5 inches is in relation to the average difference between individuals picked at random from the population. If the average difference in the population is also 1.5 inches, this means that siblings do not resemble each other in height. In fact, the average height difference for same-sex comparisons is 2.25 inches. Thus, even though sibling pairs differ in height, they are are more similar than pairs of unrelated persons. But how important is the difference between 1.5 inches and 2.25 inches?

To solve the problem of describing family resemblance, Galton, with his student Karl Pearson, invented the most important statistic in science. The *correlation coefficient* expresses sibling differences in relation to differences among individuals in the population, or more technically, indicates the extent to which variance (a statistic describing differences) among individuals covaries for siblings (see the notes for this chapter for a more detailed description). A correlation of zero denotes a complete lack of sibling resemblance, that is, siblings pairs are as different as randomly chosen pairs in the population. A correlation of 1.0 indicates that the siblings are exactly the same.

The sibling correlation for height turns out to be .50; the correlation for weight is also about .50. Roughly speaking, this means that compared to the population at large siblings are 50 percent similar. Conversely, we can focus on differences rather than similarities: the extent to which the sibling correlation is less than 1.0 denotes sibling differences. The sibling correlations for height and weight imply that siblings are 50 percent different as compared to randomly chosen pairs of individuals. As explained in the notes, it is technically more accurate to say that about half of the variance of height covaries within pairs of siblings and half of the variance does not covary. The point is that for height and weight siblings are different and similar in about equal measure.

Sibling correlations seldom exceed the correlations of .50 for height and weight. For example, sibling correlations are about .30 for distance between the eyes, height and width of the nose, and height of the ears. Big mouths run in families to the same extent—the correlation for width of mouth is also .30. About 80 percent of siblings have noticeably different eye color; 90 percent have different hair color or curliness; complexion is noticeably different for over 90 percent of sibling pairs.

Siblings resemble each other even less in their diseases. The percentage of sibling pairs in which both siblings are affected is surprisingly low for ten common diseases:

ischemic heart disease, 18% (.13)
ulcers, 15% (.10)
hypertension, 11% (.07)
breast cancer, 10% (.06)
diabetes, 8% (.06)
colon cancer, 6% (.05)

childhood eczema, 5% (.03)
rectal cancer, 3% (.02)
asthma, 4% (.07)
hay fever, 14% (.00)

The correlation figures in parentheses take into account a problem raised earlier. We noted that sibling differences in quantitative characteristics like height need to be interpreted in relation to differences among all individuals, and we face the same problem in thinking about qualitative (either-or) traits like disease. For example, does 15 percent sibling concordance for ulcers indicate similarity beyond the chance similarity of individuals selected at random?

The answer depends on the incidence of ulcers in the population at large, which is 6 percent. Thus, for ulcers, siblings are more similar than pairs picked at random from the population. But we still need to combine the 15 percent sibling concordance and the population incidence of 6 percent in order to interpret the extent of sibling similarity for ulcers. As explained in the notes, a special type of correlation (called phi) can be used to express these data as correlations that take into account population incidence in addition to pair concordance. For ulcers, the sibling correlation is then .10. For hay fever, 14 percent sibling concordance reflects a correlation of .00 because the incidence in the population is also 14 percent; pairs of siblings are no more similar for hay fever than pairs picked at random from the population. Sibling correlations for the ten diseases listed show us that different diseases strike siblings differently.

In summary, siblings differ least for height and weight, moderately for facial and other physical characteristics, and they differ most for diseases. However, even in the case of height and weight, sibling differences are as great as their similarities, as illustrated in table 1.1.

PSYCHOLOGICAL TRAITS

The range of sibling differences is also large for behavioral traits. Francis Galton was particularly interested in behavior, and one of his earliest studies focused on "superior faculties," as assessed by reputation, which would now be considered a

Table 1.1   Sibling Differences in Physical Traits and Common Diseases

	Sibling Difference (% = 1 − Correlation)										
	0	10	20	30	40	50	60	70	80	90	100
height	■■■■■■■■■■■■										
weight	■■■■■■■■■■■■										
ischemic heart disease	■■■■■■■■■■■■■■■■■■■										
ulcers	■■■■■■■■■■■■■■■■■■■										
hypertension	■■■■■■■■■■■■■■■■■■■										
breast cancer	■■■■■■■■■■■■■■■■■■■										
diabetes	■■■■■■■■■■■■■■■■■■■■										
colon cancer	■■■■■■■■■■■■■■■■■■■■										
childhood eczema	■■■■■■■■■■■■■■■■■■■■										
rectal cancer	■■■■■■■■■■■■■■■■■■■■										
asthma	■■■■■■■■■■■■■■■■■■■■										
hay fever	■■■■■■■■■■■■■■■■■■■■										

very unsatisfactory measurement tool. He studied outstanding English judges since the restoration of the monarchy (1660 to 1868), as well as statesmen, military commanders, writers, poets, scientists, musicians, and painters. As indicated in the next chapter, Galton was interested in the extent to which such abilities run in families. More specifically, his goal was to compare familial resemblance for first-, second-, and third-degree relatives (such as grandparents-grandchildren or cousins) in order to assess the importance of heredity. His study was thus the first attempt to assess sibling similarity. He referred to one in a million men (he studied only men) as "illustrious," and one in four thousand men as "eminent," and concluded:

> I reckon the chances of kinsmen of illustrious men rising, or having risen, to eminence, to be . . . 13.5 to 100 in the case of brothers.

Galton was struck by the familial resemblance (which he took to be hereditary), but we could turn this around to point out that 86.5 percent of the brothers of illustrious men were *not* eminent.

Later in his long life, Galton turned to objective measurement of behavior, putting to use his penchant for constructing gadgets, which had already led to his development of periscopes, a printing electric telegraph, and a nautical signaling device. He now invented apparatus and procedures for measuring visual acuity, auditory thresholds, reaction time, and physical strength. Galton's behavioral data yield the following same-sex sibling correlations: .19 for keenness of eyesight, .31 for highest tone heard, .35 for reaction time, and .32 for strength of squeeze.

Galton's century-old sibling correlations remain the only

ones available for these types of behavioral measures. Modern behavioral research focuses on mental abilities, personality, and mental illness. For example, IQ tests have been administered to over 25,000 pairs of siblings. The average sibling correlation for IQ scores is similar to the correlation for height and weight, .47. In other words, in comparison to IQ differences among all individuals, siblings differ at least as much as they resemble each other. In fact, siblings differ even more for IQ than these data suggest, because most of the 25,000 sibling pairs were studied as children—adult siblings differ more in IQ than do young siblings. The largest study of adult siblings reported an IQ correlation of only .31, suggesting that, by adulthood, sibling differences in IQ scores exceed similarities to a substantial degree.

A single number, the IQ score, by no means tells the whole story of mental ability. What about specific mental abilities, such as verbal facility and memory? The similarity of siblings differs for these different aspects of mental ability. Vocabulary tests yield the highest adult sibling correlations, about .35, while sibling correlations are about .25 for other verbal tests such as verbal fluency (for example, "How many words can you think of that begin with the letter g and end with the letter t?"). Sibling correlations are also about .25 for tests of spatial ability, such as visualizing the rotation of a three-dimensional object. Memory tests show even lower sibling correlations, about .15. In summary, for specific mental abilities, sibling differences far exceed their similarities.

Because siblings differ substantially in mental abilities, it is reasonable to expect that they also differ in their success at school. However, success at school involves more than pure brain power and these other factors influencing school achievement make siblings somewhat more similar in their success at school than they are in mental abilities. Sibling correlations are in general slightly greater than .50 in all fields of study.

What little is known about mental or scholastic deficiencies indicates that siblings differ substantially. For example, in about 80 percent of cases where one sibling is diagnosed as reading disabled, the other sibling is not. Mild mental retardation, indexed by IQ scores from 50 to 69, differs within sibling pairs 80 percent of the time. For severe retardation, IQ scores below 50, siblings show even greater differences—when one sibling is diagnosed as severely retarded, over 90 percent of the time the other sibling is not severely retarded. The dementia that strikes elderly people, Alzheimer's disease, is of much current interest; about 90 percent of the time, when one sibling shows the symptoms of Alzheimer's disease, the other sibling does not. Taking into account the base rates for these disorders, we obtain sibling correlations of .15 for reading disability, .19 for mild mental retardation, .10 for severe mental retardation, and .08 for Alzheimer's disease. These low sibling correlations indicate that these disorders strike children in the same family differentially.

We began with the contrasting personalities of writers and their siblings. Biographies generally—whether of writers, politicians, historical figures, film stars, or sporting successes— are replete with examples of sibling differences in personality. The term *personality* covers dozens of dimensions—such as emotionality, activity level, and sociability—which are usually measured in psychologists' research by self-report questionnaires for adults or rating instruments with which parents rate their children. Despite the diversity of definitions of personality, a simple conclusion emerges from studies in this field: siblings are remarkably different. The average sibling correlation for personality is only .15, which implies that about 85 percent of the variance in personality is not shared by two children growing up in the same family.

Consider, for example, the two "superfactors" of personality that represent major clusters of personality dimensions on which much research has focused: extraversion, encompassing such dimensions as sociability, impulsiveness, and liveliness, and neuroticism, which includes moodiness, anxiousness, and irritability in a broad dimension of emotional stability/instability. In the largest study yet completed of these traits, sibling correlations are .25 for extraversion and .07 for neuroticism.

Sibling correlations are very low for nearly all personality traits. The few exceptions reach no higher than .40 and include traits that might more properly be considered attitudes, such as masculinity-femininity, tolerance for ambiguity, and traditionalism (conformity and conservativeness). Attitudes toward racial integration show sibling resemblance of a similar magnitude. The greatest similarity documented for siblings is in religiosity (belief in deity and involvement in religious activities), a correlation of .60. What lies behind this similarity will be the topic of later chapters.

The final area that we shall consider here is mental illness and problem behavior, beginning with two general categories of severe psychopathology that have been the focus of much research. For schizophrenia, which is characterized by long-term thought disorders, hallucinations, and disorganized speech, the lifetime risk in the general population is about 1 percent. In contrast, for the subjects of thirteen studies involving nearly 10,000 siblings of schizophrenics, the risk is 10 percent. This is, of course, higher than 1 percent—but 90 percent of the siblings of schizophrenics are *not* schizophrenic.

The second category of severe mental illness involves affective or mood disorders. Unipolar depression, the most common form of mental illness, is marked by feelings of worthlessness, sadness, disturbances of sleep and appetite, loss of energy, and suicidal thoughts. A second major affective disorder is called bipolar manic-depression because it is characterized by swings from depression to mania (hyperactivity, reduced need for sleep, and euphoria). Although these disorders are difficult to diagnose because of the fine line between normal mood shifts and psychopathology, recent studies suggest that the lifetime risk for a major depressive disorder is about 5 percent, and that about 1 percent of the population has experienced both severe depressive and manic episodes. In contrast to the 5 percent risk in the general population, the risk of unipolar depression in siblings of depressed individuals is 20 percent, considerably higher for sisters (30 percent) than for brothers (10 percent). The risk for bipolar illness in siblings of individuals with bipolar illness is 6 percent; however, the risk of affective disorder in general for these siblings rises to 20 percent.

Siblings exhibit even less resemblance in less severe mental illness, such as depression in response to life events. Recent studies indicate that siblings of such depressed individuals may be no more likely to become depressed than anyone else, with a 5–10 percent risk for siblings as for the population at large. Other areas of minor mental illness show some sibling resemblance as compared to the population risks, but concordances seldom exceed 20 percent. One exception to this pattern of differences between siblings comes from the domain of deviance: in juvenile delinquency, sibling concordance is as high as 70 percent. The explanation for this high sibling resemblance may be that siblings are often partners in crime. The simple number of delinquent acts correlates .50 for young siblings, dropping to .20 by late adolescence. Adult criminality, defined by criminal records, shows concordances of 30 percent for siblings.

Finally, for alcohol abuse we see 25 percent concordance for brothers as compared to 5 percent risk for all males. Alcohol abuse is more rarely studied in women, but the concordance for sisters appears to be lower. Total amount of alcohol consumed per month correlates .30 for siblings.

As explained earlier, sibling concordances can be converted into correlations to show sibling differences in relation to base rates in the population. Sibling correlations for psychopathology are .09 for schizophrenia, .16 for unipolar depression, and .05 for bipolar manic-depression; .26 for adult criminality; and .21 for alcoholism. Table 1.2 summarizes the great extent of sibling differences for psychological traits.

The purpose of this litany of sibling data for physical and psychological traits is to convey the premise of this book—that siblings, although growing up in the same family, are remarkably different from each other. Traits do run in families but compared to the torrent of differences these similarities are only a trickle. One of the leading researchers in this field, Sandra Scarr of the University of Virginia, has made this point forcefully:

> Lest the reader slip over these results, let us make explicit the implications of these findings: Upper middle-class brothers who attend the same school and whose parents take them to the same plays, sporting events, music lessons, and therapists, and use similar child rearing practices on them are little more similar in personality measures than they are to working class or farm boys, whose lives are totally different.

Table 1.2   Sibling Differences in Psychological Traits

	Sibling Difference (% = 1 − Correlation)
	0 10 20 30 40 50 60 70 80 90 100

religiosity

school achievement

juvenile delinquent acts

traditionalism

IQ in childhood

attitudinal measures

vocabulary

IQ in adulthood

alcohol consumed monthly

verbal fluency

spatial ability

extraversion

adult criminality

alcoholism

unipolar depression

most personality traits

memory

schizophrenia

neuroticism

bipolar manic-depression

Parents and offspring differ within the family, too. Children are not just chips off the old block. Research shows that parent-offspring differences for physical and psychological traits are as great or even greater than sibling differences. However, parent-offspring differences are less surprising than sibling differences, because parents are older, of a different generation, and reared in a different family. Although it is useful to ask why parents and their offspring are so different from one another, the study of differences within pairs of siblings of similar ages reared in the same family is more incisive in exposing different lives within the family.

The challenge is to understand why siblings are so different. This is the topic of the rest of the book.

2

Differences in Nature

To see and hear them together were some of the best moments of my life, their minds the same Huxley brand of steel, their interests so much alike with the profound difference of their temperaments.
—Juliette Huxley, *Blood Brothers*

The widow of the scientist Julian Huxley comments above on the similarities and differences between her husband and his brother Aldous, the novelist. What part does heredity play in such likenesses and contrasts? When siblings differ as much as James Joyce and his brother Stanislaus—called Don Quixote and Sancho Panza by the writer Italo Svevo—has heredity contributed to their differences? James was intense, introverted, self-absorbed; Stanislaus, who acted for many years as James's audience, companion, messenger, and provider, was rough, open, and blunt, eager to please and to be liked from his childhood on. As Stanislaus saw it, "It seemed that the difference between us was not a difference of degree but of kind." Where does genetics come into the story of how sibling differences develop?

One reason why brothers and sisters are so different is heredity. The first law of heredity is that relatives are similar and the second law is that relatives are different. This is not just a convenient escape hatch for a weak theory. Rather, it is the essence of the process of inheritance, discovered over a century ago by the monk Gregor Mendel in what is now Czecho-slovakia.

MENDEL

In Mendel's time, the prevailing theory of heredity was that sperm and egg are miniature replicas of all of the cells of the mother and father. At conception, these replicas were thought to merge, producing offspring with characteristics blended from both parents. In many cases, it does seem as if children fall in between their parents. Children of a tall father and short mother are usually of middling height.

A problem with this theory of blending inheritance, which we now recognize as mistaken, is that children are often different from their parents. Short parents sometimes have tall children. Another problem—one that bedeviled Darwin in his thinking on evolution at this same time—is that blending inheritance implies that differences among people will diminish with each generation. That is, if parents who differ in height have children who are of intermediate height, a greater proportion of individuals of middling height should be observed with each passing generation. Darwin's theory of evolution depended on hereditary differences among individuals of a species: without such hereditary variability, natural selection had nothing to select. Darwin reluctantly accepted the theory of blending inheritance, for lack of an alternative, even while the solution to his problem lay in his study in a manuscript that he never opened. Although Darwin read widely, a study of peas by an unknown monk did not catch his interest.

Mendel's classic series of simple experiments showed that the theory of blending inheritance was wrong. When he crossed a variety of pea plants with smooth seeds with another variety whose seeds were wrinkled, their offspring did not develop in-between seeds that were slightly wrinkled: the seeds were smooth just like seeds of parents with smooth seeds. Blending inheritance could not explain this result.

Was the hereditary element for wrinkledness lost? Mendel answered this question by crossing these "smooth" offspring with each other. The wrinkling reappeared: one-quarter of the offspring had wrinkled seeds even though both parents had smooth seeds. Thus a theory of heredity would have to explain how like fails to beget like. The remaining three-quarters of these offspring had smooth seeds. This indicates that heredity makes siblings different, if we think of the smooth and wrinkled peas of this last generation as siblings.

The same three-to-one ratio emerged when Mendel conducted similar experiments with other characteristics of the pea plant, such as crossing a short-stemmed variety with a long-stemmed variety. Moreover, Mendel showed that when this three-to-one generation is bred, the next generation also yields the three-to-one ratio. In fact, all subsequent generations yield this same three-to-one ratio in the absence of forces selectively favoring the reproduction of one type. This important finding implies that heredity maintains genetic variability generation after generation.

How can these results be explained? Mendel concluded that inheritance involves two "elements," one from each parent. These elements are discrete and independent—they do not blend. In addition, he argued, one element can dominate the other in the sense that the dominant element is expressed but the recessive element is not. These two suppositions can explain the three-to-one ratios that Mendel found in his experiments (see figure 2.1). In the case of the cross between smooth-seeded and wrinkled-seeded varieties, suppose that the hereditary element for smoothness is dominant and the element for wrinkling is recessive. The first-generation offspring will each have one element for smooth seeds and one for wrinkled seeds, but all of their seeds will be smooth because the element for smooth seeds is dominant. When these individuals are crossed with each other, the next generation will consist of equal portions of individuals with smooth-smooth, smooth-wrinkled, wrinkled-smooth, and wrinkled-wrinkled pairs of elements. If the smooth element is dominant, the first three types will all have smooth seeds. Only the fourth type, the wrinkled-

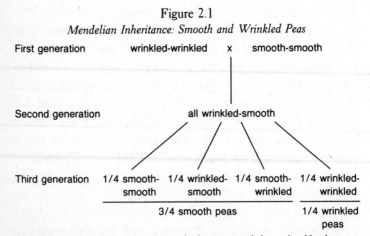

Figure 2.1
Mendelian Inheritance: Smooth and Wrinkled Peas

First generation   wrinkled-wrinkled   x   smooth-smooth

Second generation   all wrinkled-smooth

Third generation   1/4 smooth-smooth   1/4 wrinkled-smooth   1/4 smooth-wrinkled   1/4 wrinkled-wrinkled

3/4 smooth peas   1/4 wrinkled peas

Mendel's experiment led to his theory of inheritance and shows that like does not beget like. That is, heredity makes siblings different from one another as well as similar to each other.

wrinkled individuals, will have wrinkled seeds. This is the three-to-one ratio that Mendel observed in his experiments.

For our purpose, Mendel's theory is important because it provides the basis for understanding that heredity predicts sibling differences as well as sibling similarities. If blending inheritance were correct, all offspring should be intermediate to their mother and father. Siblings then would not differ. Mendel's theory, however, shows that siblings can be expected to differ in hereditary traits. Because parents each have two elements and offspring inherit one element from each parent, siblings have only a fifty-fifty chance of inheriting the same element.

AFTER MENDEL

Not only did Mendel's work escape Darwin's attention, it was ignored for forty years by the entire scientific community. Mendel died not knowing the impact that his theory would have on biology when it was rediscovered at the turn of the twentieth century. Mendel's hereditary elements are now called genes. Random mutation, error in copying genes, is considered the ultimate source of different forms of genes, called alleles, which complete Darwin's theory of evolution: genetic variability is not blended away during inheritance, but remains generation after generation unless natural selection intervenes to affect the reproductive success of one type over another.

A decade-long debate ensued when Mendel's theory was rediscovered. Was the theory limited to certain characteristics of plants or did it describe how heredity works even for complex traits in the human species? Most human characteristics are not qualitative, either-or traits like those studied by Mendel in the pea plant. For example, people may indeed be wrinkled or smooth, short or tall, but these are not exclusive alternatives. As with beauty or brain power, skin texture and height are distributed between people in a bell-shaped curve (called a normal distribution) in which most people are in the middle, and the farther from the middle we look, the fewer individuals we find. The normal distribution for height is shown in figure 2.2, as assessed by Galton in his nineteenth-century study.

The debate was resolved with the insight that many genes

Figure 2.2
Normal Distribution for Height

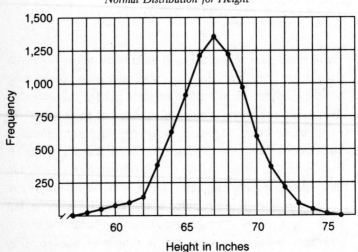

Height, as well as most psychological traits, is normally distributed in a bell-shaped curve in which most people score in the middle and fewer people are found toward either end of the distribution. These data on height were collected by Francis Galton for 8,585 adult men in England during the nineteenth century. Modern data show the same normal distribution but the average is higher.

can affect a trait. If several genes, each with a small effect, contribute to a trait's variability, a normal distribution will result even though each gene is inherited in the qualitative manner described by Mendel. Behavioral dimensions and disorders are affected by many genes, each with small effects, unlike the single-gene characteristics that Mendel studied in peas. This is not surprising. Behavior is obviously very complex, in that it is dynamic, changing in response to the environment. While no single-gene or even major-gene effects have been demonstrated for behavior other than rare mutations that drastically disrupt normal development, causing, for example, mental retardation, each of many genes affecting behavior can be transmitted hereditarily according to Mendel's laws in the same way that genes affect any other phenotype.

The argument that many genes affect behavior might seem to fly in the face of reports in the past two years that "the gene" for bipolar manic-depression or for schizophrenia has been found. These reports were based on studies that correlate the inheritance of genetic markers with the inheritance of a disorder within a family. If the traits are inherited together, they must be linked on the same chromosome. Linkage analysis has aided in identifying the chromosomal location for Huntington's chorea, polycystic kidney disease, cystic fibrosis, Duchenne muscular dystrophy, and half a dozen other diseases. These are disorders that have long been known to be caused by a single gene that takes its toll regardless of a person's other genes or environment. Current linkage studies can only detect a gene that is largely responsible for a disorder, but the inheritance of behavioral disorders, including bipolar manic-depression and schizophrenia, is much more complicated. How, then, was linkage found for bipolar manic-depression and schizophrenia? The answer is, it wasn't. The report of linkage for bipolar manic-depression has been withdrawn, and repeated efforts to replicate the reported linkage for schizophrenia have failed. Molecular genetics, by far the fastest-moving field of science today, will eventually be able to address complex phenotypes, such as behavior, that are influenced by many genes each with small effects as well as by nongenetic factors. For the present, however, investigations of genetic influence must rely on the less direct strategies of quantitative genetics that were developed during the early part of this century.

HEREDITARY RESEMBLANCE BETWEEN RELATIVES

In addition to resolving the problem of inheritance of quantitative characteristics, geneticists in the early part of this century worked out the degree of resemblance to be expected for various relatives when many genes affect a trait. Correlation, an index of resemblance described in the previous chapter, was developed by Francis Galton and his student Karl Pearson for the purpose of assessing familial resemblance. Ironically, this statistic was first applied by Galton to a characteristic of the sweet pea long before Mendel's work on the edible pea had been rediscovered. Unlike the qualitative traits that Mendel studied, Galton chose to study seed size, measured by diameter, a quantitative trait that is normally distributed.

Pearson's student Ronald Fisher showed that siblings are 50 percent similar genetically in the sense that, when alleles vary between individuals, siblings have a fifty-fifty chance of inheriting the same allele. Although geneticists focus on hereditary resemblance, in the present context the opposite side of that same coin is more relevant: siblings are 50 percent different genetically. The 50 percent is only on average. Human genes come packaged in twenty-three pairs of chromosomes; one member of each pair of chromosomes comes from the mother and the other from the father. Siblings have a fifty-fifty chance of inheriting a different chromosome for each member of each pair of chromosomes. If siblings inherit different chromosomes, they inherit the package of thousands of different alleles that may be on that chromosome. In this way, luck of the draw could make some siblings less similar genetically and others more similar. Actually, this is less of a factor than it might seem, because chromosomes from mothers and fathers recombine, exchanging parts, so that siblings rarely inherit exactly the same chromosome.

Overall, heredity contributes more to differences than to similarities between siblings. Fisher noted that genetic relatedness of .50 for siblings rests on the assumption that genetic effects on a trait are additive. For example, if one gene contributes an average effect of 1 and another gene's effect is also 1, their combined effect is 2. Genes do not always operate in this manner—1 plus 1 may not equal 2. Particular combinations of genes may have nonadditive (interactive) effects. For example, the particular combination of genes just described may have an effect of 4 rather than 2. Dominance is a type of nonadditive effect within a single gene which occurs when there is no difference between having just one dominant allele or two. In Mendel's studies, hybrid offspring with one dominant allele for smooth seeds had seeds just as smooth as their true-breeding parents who had two dominant alleles for smoothness. Another nonadditive effect, called epistasis, involves interactions among different genes. Such nonadditive genetic effects contribute only slightly to resemblance of siblings because siblings have little chance of inheriting exactly the same combinations of genes, especially when many genes affect a trait. Thus, if nonadditive genetic effects are important, heredity contributes more to sibling differences than to their similarities. There is some evidence to suggest that genetic effects are nonadditive for behavior, especially for personality and psychopathology. We can detect nonadditive genetic variance through comparisons with identical twins, who are identical for all genetic effects, including interactions among many genes. Thus, the hallmark of nonadditive genetic variance is the case in which identical twins resemble each other but first-degree relatives do not.

Of course, if heredity does not affect a trait, then none of this matters. If heredity is unimportant for a particular trait, genetic factors contribute neither to differences nor similarities of siblings. On the other hand, if heredity accounts for all of the similarities and differences of siblings, then there is no need to consider environmental factors. How large is the role played by heredity?

NATURE AND NURTURE

The relative importance of nature (heredity) and nurture (environment) is one of the oldest issues in the behavioral sciences. Toward the end of the nineteenth century, Francis Galton, who popularized the phrase *nature and nurture,* showed that many complex traits such as beauty, brawn, and brains run in families. He believed that familial resemblance was primarily genetic in origin, but he had no methods available to prove it. Familial resemblance could, of course, be due to nurture just as easily as to nature. If we find that fat parents have fat children and grandchildren, is this because they have similar eating patterns or similar genetic makeup?

Adoption and Twin Studies

Two methods of disentangling the effects of nature and nurture were developed in the 1920s: adoption and twin studies. Adoption cleaves nature and nurture because it results in relatives who share heredity but not family environment (biological relatives adopted apart) and in relatives who share family environment but not heredity (genetically unrelated individuals adopted together). If heredity is important, relatives should be similar even when they are adopted apart. If family environment is responsible for relatives' similarity, genetically unrelated individuals adopted together should resemble each other.

Twin studies compare samples of identical and fraternal twins. By the turn of the century, embryological research indicated that there are two types of twins. For two-thirds of the twins, two eggs are released and both are fertilized. These twins, called dizygotic (two zygotes), or fraternal, are siblings who happen to be born at the same time. Monozygotic, or identical, twins derive from a single fertilized egg that divides into two separate zygotes during the first few days after conception. Both types of twins are similar in many ways. They both develop prenatally in the same womb, they are the same age, and they may grow up in the same family.

The two types of twins differ in one dramatic way: fraternal twins are at least twice as different genetically as identical twins. That is, identical twins are identical genetically, whereas fraternal twins are siblings who are, as discussed earlier, genetically related on average as much as 50 percent. If a particular trait is influenced by heredity, fraternal twins will show greater differences than identical twins. If heredity is unimportant, the twofold greater genetic similarity of identical twins will make no difference, and fraternal twins will be as similar as identical twins.

In summary, if a trait is influenced by heredity, we would expect adopted-apart relatives to resemble each other. We would also expect biological siblings reared in the same families to be more similar than genetically unrelated "siblings" adopted into the same families. In twin studies, we would expect to find identical twins to be more similar than fraternal twins. If heredity is unimportant, adopted-apart relatives will not resemble each other, biological siblings will be no more similar than adoptive siblings, and identical twins will be no more similar than fraternal twins.

In addition to indicating whether genetic factors significantly affect quantitative traits, adoption and twin data can be used to estimate the size of the effect. For example, genetic factors account for all of the variance of a trait if the correlation for first-degree relatives adopted apart is .50, if biological siblings correlate .50 and adoptive siblings correlate .00, and if identical twins and fraternal twins correlate 1.0 and .50, respectively. For no behavior, however, does heredity account for all variance—as we shall see, its influence is generally much less. If heredity accounts for half the variance, first-degree relatives adopted apart should correlate .25, biological siblings should correlate at least .25, and identical and fraternal twins should correlate at least .50 and .25, respectively. The notes for this chapter describe heritability, an estimate of the size of the genetic effect, in greater detail. We wish to emphasize that heritability is merely a descriptive statistic that indicates for a particular population at a particular time the extent to which genetic differences among individuals can account for observed differences. It is not an immutable constant, nor does it tell us how genes have their effect.

From the previous chapter it should be clear that sibling differences outweigh sibling similarities for most physical and psychological traits. This tells us that heredity cannot explain all sibling differences, because if that were so, sibling correlations should be nearer .50 on the basis of their 50 percent shared heredity. If we knew how much heredity affects these traits, we could estimate the extent to which sibling differences are due to hereditary differences. Of course, if genetic influence is zero for a particular trait, none of the sibling difference for that trait is due to heredity. In contrast, suppose that heredity accounts for 40 percent of the variance for a particular trait. This implies that siblings will be different 20 percent on the basis of heredity alone.

Evidence for Genetic Influence

What about differences in physical appearance, such as differences in height and weight? Photographs of Katherine Mansfield's family show her as a plump, plain child, while her sisters were beautiful, tall, and slim; the Joyce brothers were dubbed Don Quixote and Sancho Panza; and descriptions of D. H. Lawrence and his brothers contrast George (short, handsome, with regular features) and Ernest (strongly built and "taking after his father") with David Herbert (thin and frail). "With ginger hair and a face like chalk, he was the most effeminate boy I knew," a schoolmate commented.

The part that heredity plays in such differences is, not surprisingly, great. Differences in height, for instance, occur primarily (about 80 percent) for genetic reasons. The simplest adoption study design is the rare but dramatic situation in which identical twins are adopted separately at birth and reared apart in uncorrelated environments. The resemblance of these pairs, expressed as a correlation, can be attributed directly to heredity, as explained in the notes. The correlation for reared-apart identical twins for height is .80, which suggests that 80 percent of the variance of height is due to heredity. For adopted-apart first-degree relatives height correlates about .40, which again suggests that 80 percent of the variance in height is due to genetic factors. Height correlates .90 for identical twins reared together; for fraternal twins about .50. These twin comparisons also indicate that 80 percent of the variance in height is genetic in origin.

In this example, 80 percent heritability also means that 80 percent of the difference between siblings is heritable. As shown in the previous chapter, siblings are 50 percent different in height. Heritability of 80 percent implies that siblings will be 40 percent different on the basis of heredity alone. In other words, 80 percent (that is, 40 percent of 50 percent) of sibling differences in height are due to genetic differences.

Sibling differences in weight are almost as much a function of genetic factors as are differences in height. In adulthood, identical and fraternal twin correlations are .80 and .50, respectively. This suggests that 60 percent of the weight difference among individuals is due to genetic differences and that 60 percent (that is, 30 percent of 50 percent) of the weight difference of siblings is also due to heredity. It is also clear that differences between siblings in other physical characteristics are chiefly caused by genetic differences. For example, in the previous chapter, we mentioned that siblings show considerable differences in eye color, hair color, and complexion. Identical twins are virtually identical in these characteristics, suggesting that sibling differences in these traits are entirely genetic in origin.

Common diseases such as heart disease and cancers strike siblings quite differentially as we saw in the last chapter. Table 2.1 repeats the overview of sibling differences in physical traits and common diseases from the previous chapter, adding the extent to which sibling differences can be attributed to genetic factors. In the case of height and weight, most sibling differ-

Table 2.1 Origins of Sibling Differences in Physical Traits and Common Diseases
("-" indicates genetic effect, "X" denotes nongenetic effect.)

	Sibling Difference (% = 1 − Correlation)										
	0	10	20	30	40	50	60	70	80	90	100
height	------------------------XXX										
weight	--------------------XXXXX										
ischemic heart disease	------XXXXXXXXXXXXXXXXXXXX										
ulcers	-----XXXXXXXXXXXXXXXXXXXXX										
hypertension	--------XXXXXXXXXXXXXXXXXXXXX										
breast cancer	-XXXXXXXXXXXXXXXXXXXXXXXXX										
diabetes	----XXXXXXXXXXXXXXXXXXXXXXX										
colon cancer	-XXXXXXXXXXXXXXXXXXXXXXXXXX										
childhood eczema	---XXXXXXXXXXXXXXXXXXXXXXXXX										
rectal cancer	-XXXXXXXXXXXXXXXXXXXXXXXXXX										
asthma	----XXXXXXXXXXXXXXXXXXXXXXXX										
hay fever	---XXXXXXXXXXXXXXXXXXXXXXXXXX										

ences are due to genetics, but, for common diseases, genetics plays a much smaller role. For example, identical and fraternal twin correlations are, respectively, .24 and .13 for heart disease, .08 and .06 for breast cancer, and .19 and .10 for ulcers. On average, less than 7 percent of the sibling differences for the diseases listed in table 2.1 can be accounted for by genetic differences between siblings.

For psychological traits, a larger portion of the differences between siblings are accounted for by genetic differences than is the case for common diseases, as illustrated in table 2.2. Some aspects of peoples' attitudes, such as their religiosity, show no genetic influence, but on average about one-third of the difference between siblings in psychological features is due to genetic factors. The most extensively studied trait is IQ. The correlation between "genetic" parents and their adopted-away offspring is about .25. Adopted-apart siblings also correlate about .25. What these figures imply is that 50 percent of the variance between individuals in their IQ scores is due to hereditary influences. The findings from studies of twins are similar: identical twin correlations are about .25 greater than fraternal twin correlations (.85 versus .60).

Taken together, these findings make it difficult to escape the conclusion that heredity significantly influences individual differences in IQ scores. Estimates of the extent of genetic influence on IQ scores cluster around 50 percent. Half of siblings' differences in IQ can be ascribed to heredity. In the previous chapter, we noted that siblings increasingly differ in IQ with development from childhood to adulthood. However, genetic differences account for roughly the same proportion of these IQ differences in childhood and adulthood. Although less thoroughly studied than IQ, adoption and twin data for the other domains listed in table 2.2 converge on the conclusion that

Table 2.2 Origins of Sibling Difference in Psychological Traits ("-" indicates genetic effect, "X" denotes nongenetic effect.)

```
                          Sibling Difference (% = 1 − Correlation)
                     0   10  20  30  40  50  60  70  80  90  100

religiosity          XXXXXXXXXX
school achievement   ----------XXXXXXXX
juvenile delinquent
acts                 -------------XXXXXXX
traditionalism       -------XXXXXXXXXX
IQ in childhood      ---------------XXXXXXX
vocabulary           -----------XXXXXXXXXXX
IQ in adulthood      ----------------XXXXXXXXXX
alcohol consumed
monthly              --------------------------XXXXX
verbal fluency       ---------XXXXXXXXXXXXXX
spatial ability      --------------XXXXXXXXXXXX
extraversion         ----------------XXXXXXXXXXX
adult criminality    --------------------XXXXXXXXXX
depression           ---------------------XXXXXXXXXXXX
most personality
traits               ----------------XXXXXXXXXXXXXX
memory               ----------XXXXXXXXXXXXXXXXX
schizophrenia        -----------XXXXXXXXXXXXXXXXXX
neuroticism          ------------------XXXXXXXXXXXXXX
```

heredity significantly and substantially affects many aspects of behavior. The magnitude of genetic influence varies. Some types of memory ability, for example, appear to show less genetic influence than other types of mental ability. Extraversion and neuroticism are more heritable than other aspects of personality. The most important feature of table 2.2, however, is that about one-third of the difference between siblings is due to genetic factors.

Ten or fifteen years ago, the relevant message conveyed by the information in table 2.2 was that heredity affects behavior. Now, however, the message that is needed as an antidote for the recent swing toward biological determinism is this: although heredity substantially affects behavior, nongenetic factors are at least as important. For example, the reason why one person is diagnosed schizophrenic and another is not has more to do with nongenetic than genetic factors. Identical twin concordance for schizophrenia is less than 50 percent, which means that in more than half the cases where one member of an identical-twin pair is schizophrenic the genetically identical twin is not. In relation to siblings, these findings for schizophrenia—and for other psychological traits—indicate that heredity contributes importantly to sibling differences. Some two-thirds of the sibling differences remain to be explained by nongenetic factors.

What accounts for the rest of the sibling differences? A simple answer is the environment. We use the word *environment* to refer to any nonhereditary influence on development. It is not limited to the psychosocial environmental factors such as interactions with family members that tend to be the focus of attention in the social and behavioral sciences. Our broader definition includes nonhereditary biological factors such as illness and accidents, nutrition, and even events related to DNA itself. For example, DNA is thought to be importantly involved in the failure of mechanisms to control the rapid cell growth that leads to cancer, perhaps because of viral infections that take over the genetic control of cells. These are nonhereditary DNA events—as indicated in this chapter, cancer shows little genetic influence in the sense of hereditary effects transmitted from one generation to the next.

The means whereby environment causes sibling differences that are not explained by heredity are not simple; how they operate is the topic of the next chapter. In chapters 4 to 6 we will emphasize psychosocial environmental factors and in chapter 7 we will consider nonhereditary biological factors.

3

Differences in Nurture

The best available evidence that genetic factors are importantly involved in the creation of sibling differences in behavior comes from adoption and twin studies, as the previous chapter showed. Paradoxically, these same results document the importance of nongenetic factors: most sibling differences, especially in psychological traits, are not explained by genetic differences between the individuals. Hidden in these findings is an implication that revolutionizes how we think about the environmental origins of behavior. The argument so far can be expressed most clearly as a syllogism: 1) If siblings are so different, and 2) if genetic factors account for only a small portion of these differences, then 3) nongenetic factors must be primarily responsible for sibling differences. We now take this argument farther: nearly all environmental influences operate to make siblings growing up in the same family different, not similar. The implication is this: environmental factors important to development are those that two children in the same family experience differently. In other words, either families make siblings different or they have no effect on their development.

How can families make siblings different? After all, siblings grow up in the same family. But is it really the *same* family?

Although siblings have the same parents, usually eat the same foods, and often go to the same schools, when we look closer, we find that many experiences in the family are in fact different for siblings. Siblings are treated differently by their parents and by their siblings and, even if their treatment seems to be similar, they may experience it very differently. The point of later chapters will be to show that siblings live different lives even though they grow up in the same family. First we will document our argument that environmental influences important in development must be those that make children in the same family different.

This is a revolutionary concept because it contradicts much of the received wisdom about how the environment affects development. Since Freud's interpretation of how family experiences influence personality and adjustment, psychologists have generally assumed that the differences that matter vary from family to family. A mother's own childhood experience will color her mothering, it is supposed—and that means the mothering of *all* her children. If a man had a stressful relationship with his father, it is assumed that this may affect his fathering and that it will do so in the same way for *all* his children.

This perspective dominates the study of development. Psychologists who want to understand such environmental influences have set out to make comparisons *between* families. The typical psychological study attempts to analyze environmental influence by correlating measures of the family environment (or the parents' earlier experiences) and measures of children's development. For example, consider the influence of parents. Some parents are permissive and others are authoritarian. Much research into possible parental influence consists of correlating differences in parental style across families measured by the developmental outcome of one child per family. This seems a reasonable approach to discover whether parental permissiveness is related to differences in children's development, but we should note that it implies an assumption that children in the same family experience the same family environment. An implication of this tacit assumption is that it is average differences *between* family environments that are critical in creating differences among children. Because this assumption seems so reasonable, it was not examined critically until it became clear that research based on it was largely coming up empty-handed, as we discuss in the notes.

The import of what we are saying is that this traditional view is wrong. To the extent that any environmental factor, such as parental permissiveness, is shared by children in the same family, it *cannot* be important in development. The reason that an environmental factor shared by siblings cannot be important is that, if it were important, it would make siblings similar as compared to siblings in other families. As we will see in the next section, however, experiences within the family do not make siblings similar. The only factors important to children's development are those that are experienced differently by children in the same family. Although environmental factors differ from family to family, these are not important in development unless they also happen to differ within a family. In other words, environmental influences that affect development operate on an individual-by-individual basis, not on a family-by-family basis. The conclusion is inescapable and its far-reaching significance flips the nature-nurture issue from figure to ground—from a focus on heredity, to a focus on environment.

Although this implication escaped notice for decades in the glare of nature-nurture arguments, it stares at us from the data reviewed in the previous chapter, as we see in the following section.

THE IMPORTANCE OF NONSHARED ENVIRONMENT IN HUMAN DEVELOPMENT

We can go beyond the findings of the previous chapters to assert that growing up in the same family does not at all make siblings similar. For decades, we were misled by resemblance within families. Because heredity was not given its due, it was assumed that sibling similarity is caused by environmental factors shared by children growing up in the same family. The data described in the previous chapter imply that siblings resemble each other for genetic reasons, however, not for environmental reasons. That is, siblings are similar, but they are just as similar if they are adopted apart and reared in different families. Growing up in the same family is not responsible for their resemblance. What runs in families is DNA, not shared experiences in the family.

How do we know that shared environment is of so little importance? Biological siblings, of course, share both family environment and heredity and, for this reason, we cannot assess the relative importance of nature and nurture in their similarity. Two answers implicit in the previous chapters provide indirect evidence. First, shared environmental influence would by definition make siblings similar but, as we saw in chapter 1, siblings are *not* very similar, especially psychologically. Second, as we have just noted, the similarity between siblings can be completely explained by heredity, and this

43

leaves no room for shared environmental influence as an explanation of sibling resemblance.

A direct test of the extent to which shared family experiences make children in the same family similar involves studying adoptive siblings, genetically unrelated children adopted into the same families early in life. Because these siblings are not genetically related, their similarity can be caused only by shared family environment. The correlation between adoptive siblings for any particular feature of their development indicates the total impact of all shared environmental factors that make individuals growing up in the same family similar to one another in that feature. If adoptive brothers are alike, this cannot be due to genetic similarity. If they are different, it suggests that either genetic factors are important or that their shared family world is affecting them differently.

Twin studies can also be used to estimate the influence of shared and nonshared environment. The difference within pairs of identical twins provides a direct estimate of nonshared environment because identical twins are identical genetically and thus differ only for environmental reasons. This estimate of nonshared environment based on identical twins will be lower than estimates using other methods if identical twins experience more similar environments than other siblings. Shared environment can be assessed indirectly as twin resemblance that cannot be explained by heredity. Typically in twin studies, nonshared environment is assessed as the remainder of the variance that cannot be ascribed to heredity or to shared environment. The correlation for adoptive siblings provides a more direct test of the importance of shared environment.

Height and weight provide a simple example. Height and weight differences between siblings (such as those between the Mansfield sisters or the Joyce brothers) are, as we saw in the last chapter, strongly influenced by heredity. The study of adoptive siblings directly assesses the importance of shared environmental influences on height and weight. The results of adoption studies show that growing up in the same family does not make adoptive siblings at all similar—their correlation is nearly zero. From this finding we can conclude that shared environmental influences are of no importance for height and weight and this in turn means that nonshared environmental influence accounts for *all* the variation that is not hereditary. Although this finding is not surprising for height, the fact that growing up in the same family does not make siblings similar for weight is startling in the context of prevailing theories, which see nutritional and life-style patterns in the family as particularly important in explaining weight. Similarity in siblings' height and weight (think of the elegant Virginia Woolf and her sister Vanessa) is genetic in origin and not due to their shared family world.

Figures 3.1 and 3.2 show the components of variance from the data from the previous chapters in pie charts. Rather than talking about the percentages of sibling differences that are due to genetic and nongenetic factors, we can address the more general issue of variance among all individuals in the population. For example, as described in chapter 2, the heritability of height is 80 percent, which means that 80 percent of the difference (variance) among people is due to genetic differences among them. Thus, only 20 percent of the variance in height is not accounted for by heredity. The rest of the variance is nongenetic, derived, specifically, from the nonshared environment rather than shared environment. (Error of measurement is unimportant for height.) For weight, heritability is about 60 percent. The surprise is that none of the remaining 40 percent of the variance in weight is due to shared environ-

Figure 3.1
Components of Variance in Height

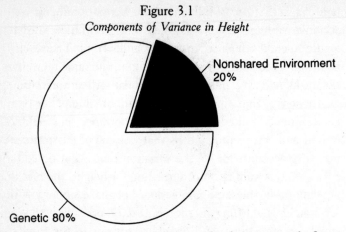

Nonshared Environment
20%

Genetic 80%

The variance of height is due primarily to genetic factors; environmental influence is entirely nonshared.

Figure 3.2
Components of Variance in Weight

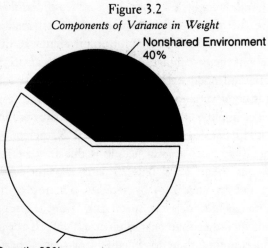

Nonshared Environment
40%

Genetic 60%

The variance of weight is due primarily to genetic factors; environmental influence is entirely nonshared.

ment. As in the case of height, all of the environmental variance is nonshared. Estimates of genetic and environmental components of such variance are shrouded in some guesswork; for example, the genetic component of variance in weight could be as high as 70 percent or as low as 50 percent. Nonetheless, these pie charts for height and weight differences highlight and summarize our argument: genetic influence is substantial, as is nonshared environment, but shared environment is of no importance.

Because siblings differ so much in the incidence of common diseases (see table 1.1), it should not be surprising that what is shared in the family environment has negligible effects in this domain. Genetic effects on common diseases are modest, and so we are left with nonshared environmental influences as the major explanation of such diseases, as illustrated in figure 3.3. In other words, because neither heredity nor shared environment affect siblings' susceptibility to disease, the main answer to the question why one individual contracts a disease and another does not must lie in environmental influences that are not shared by the siblings. For diseases caused by infection, this conclusion is not surprising; it may be a matter of chance whether an individual encounters a source of infection. The diseases listed in chapter 2—heart disease, ulcers, cancers, asthma—are unlikely to be caused by infections; our understanding of the environmental causes and cures of these diseases can only be furthered by recognizing that the causes are not environmental causes that vary family by family but rather those that differ *within* families. Because these diseases occur in adulthood after siblings have led different lives outside their family, it makes sense that differences between siblings—such as differences in smoking, diet, and life-style—are responsible for sibling differences in the incidence of these diseases. To the

Figure 3.3
Components of Variance in Common Diseases

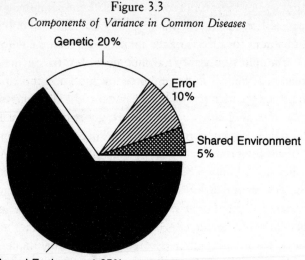

The variance of common medical diseases shows modest genetic influence; most of the variance is due to nonshared environment.

extent that these diseases have their roots earlier in life, in the family, we must seek these roots in familial differences in the siblings' experiences, not in experiences shared by siblings. To what extent are the diets of siblings, and their budding lifestyles different? We know next to nothing just because the family has for so long been thought of as a monolithic unit of experience its members share in common.

The story is much the same for psychological traits. Adoptive siblings scarcely resemble each other in personality. The average correlation for self-report personality questionnaires for adoptive siblings is .05, suggesting that growing up in the same family accounts for only about 5 percent of the variance of personality traits. Studies of nearly all personality traits yield this same result. Only some attitudes and beliefs, such as aspects of masculinity-femininity and religious and political beliefs, show the effects of the influence of shared environment.

For most personality traits, identical and fraternal twin correlations are .50 and .30, respectively. Thus the difference between the identical twin correlation and 1.0 is .50. What this means is that 50 percent of the variance is not shared by identical twins. Heritability is estimated as 40 percent (doubling the difference between the identical and fraternal twin correlations). Shared environment is estimated to account for 10 percent (identical twin correlation of .50 minus the .40 estimate of heritability). This twin estimate of 10 percent for shared environment is greater than the more direct estimate from pairs of genetically unrelated individuals reared together. It makes some sense that twins share more experiences than do non-twin siblings, because twins are exactly the same age.

Figure 3.4 illustrates these components of variance in personality. Genetic influence is appreciable, and error of measurement is certainly greater than for height and weight and probably greater than for common medical diseases. Nearly all of the environmental variance is of the nonshared variety.

In the area of psychopathology, adoptive siblings have only rarely been studied. For schizophrenia, the evidence indicates that adoptive siblings of a person who suffers from schizophrenia are at no greater risk for schizophrenia than those with normal siblings, even though they grew up in the same family with the person who later became schizophrenic. Data on twins, which are more plentiful, agree with the conclusion that shared family environment is not important. For example, differences within pairs of identical twins can only be caused by nongenetic factors. And identical twins are less than 50 percent similar for schizophrenia. This finding implies that the

Figure 3.4
Components of Variance in Personality

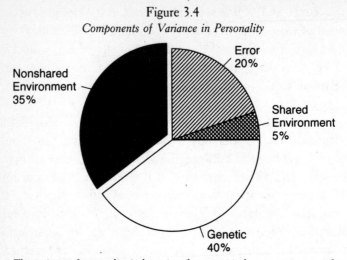

The variance of personality is due primarily to genetic factors; environmental influence is almost entirely nonshared.

major reason why one person is diagnosed as schizophrenic and another is not must be the impact of environmental influence that is not shared by family members.

Studies that compare biological parents and their adopted-away offspring with parents who rear their own children tell the same story. The risk for schizophrenia in the children of schizophrenics is just as great when such children are not reared by their schizophrenic parent. Although it is more difficult to estimate components of variance for a disorder such as schizophrenia than for personality (which we can measure in a quantitative fashion), rough approximations are illustrated in figure 3.5. The results are very similar to those for personality. Genetic influence is appreciable, and nearly all of the environmental variance is of the nonshared variety. Shared family environment has little to do with schizophrenia.

Figure 3.5

Components of Variance in Schizophrenia

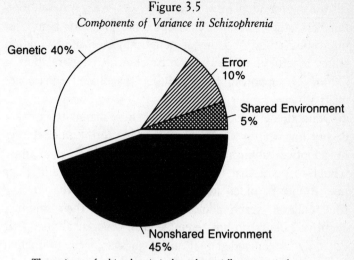

The variance of schizophrenia is due substantially to genetic factors; environmental influence is almost entirely nonshared.

Although no other type of mental illness has been studied as thoroughly as schizophrenia, what little evidence exists—for example, on depression, alcoholism, and criminality—is in line with the conclusion that the effective environmental influences are not shared by siblings growing up in the same family. One exception might be juvenile delinquency, although only twin studies have been reported on this topic, and it is likely that adolescent twins are more often partners in crime than nontwin siblings, who on average differ in age by two years.

What about intelligence? Surely children brought up together with the same educational advantages or disadvantages will show some similarity due to their shared experiences? Until recently, it seemed that shared experiences within the family in the early years importantly influence siblings' IQ. The IQ correlation for adoptive siblings is .32 on average. In addition to several studies of children adopted into the same family, an interesting study of pairs of genetically unrelated children reared together on kibbutzim in Israel yielded a correlation of .29 for IQ, supporting the conclusion that shared experiences make siblings similar in IQ.

Dramatic new results suggest that these shared experiences do not importantly affect IQ in the long run. Earlier studies of adoptive siblings all involved children in elementary school—a point that had not been seen as significant. Four new studies of older adoptive siblings indicate that by the time children reach adolescence and leave their families, adoptive siblings do not resemble each other at all in IQ. It can only be concluded that, although shared environmental influence affects IQ in childhood, its influence drops to negligible levels after childhood. A recent analysis of all published twin data for IQ also suggests that shared environmental influence declines during the life course. In other words, parental encouragement might have a similar effect on the IQ scores of two young children in the same family, but such variables have no long-term effect on IQ after childhood. (See figure 3.6.) In summary, after childhood, genetic and environmental components of variance for IQ are similar to those for other psychological traits: there is substantial genetic influence and nonshared environmental influence but little effect of shared family environment.

When we examine particular aspects of cognitive ability, such as verbal ability or memory, the results suggest that shared environment may exert some long-term effect on verbal abilities, especially vocabulary, and on school achievement. Even here, however, nonshared environmental influence outweighs shared environment.

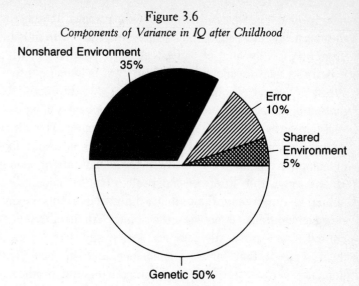

Figure 3.6

Components of Variance in IQ after Childhood

The variance of IQ scores after childhood is due substantially to genetic factors; environmental variance is almost entirely nonshared.

NONSHARED ENVIRONMENT IN ANIMALS

Although we are especially aware of sibling differences in our own species, siblings are just as different in other animals, and nonshared environment is just as important in the creation of sibling differences. Indeed, nonprimate mammals show even more dramatic sibling differences because they typically have litters of multiple twin births. For example, despite the restricted genetic variance within a dog breed, pups in the same litter can be extraordinarily different, especially in their personality and intelligence. This is a point close to home for us. Our golden retriever, Charley, is a large, lumbering, placid fellow.

We could almost have called him Slow-and-Solid, following the Kipling story. His sister Molly, who belongs to our friend and neighbor, is a dynamo of endless, agitated activity. We have to stick to such anecdotal material for most mammals, as they are rarely studied from this perspective. But the reports of sibling differences are striking, even for elephant siblings!

More systematically studied is the house mouse. As in other mammals, large differences between littermates have been documented. Even more impressive is the magnitude of sibling differences within litters of genetically identical mice called inbred strains because these sibling differences cannot be due to genetic differences between the siblings. All members of an inbred strain are nearly identical genetically, like identical twins (except that inbred strains include both males and females), because they have been inbred by mating brother to sister for at least twenty generations. Inbreeding increases the chances that for a particular gene the same allele (alternate form of a gene) will be inherited from mother and father. This is the reason that inbreeding is prohibited in most human societies. We are all carriers for several debilitating and even lethal alleles that rarely exert any effect because the genes are recessive. (Dominant alleles would be eliminated quickly by natural selection.) If two carriers mate, however, one-quarter of their offspring can inherit a double dose of the allele and thus show the recessive trait. Matings between carriers are much more likely to occur in genetically related individuals. For this reason, attempts to create inbred strains of mice frequently fail as inbreeding proceeds to lock on to deleterious alleles. By chance, inbreeding sometimes avoids locking on to bad genes and a viable inbred strain is created.

Over one hundred inbred strains of mice are available that are genetically different from one another. The average differences between genetically different inbred strains reared in the same controlled laboratory conditions strikingly illustrate the importance of heredity. Much less attention has been given to the fact that littermates within an inbred strain are very different behaviorally, even though they are genetically identical and reared in the same laboratory conditions. Differences among genetically identical littermates can only be due to nonshared environment. Ironically, some evidence exists that shared "family" environment may be more important for mouse personality than for human personality. For example, an important dimension of mouse personality is how adventurous a mouse is, shown by its exploratory behavior in novel settings. An explicit comparison within and between litters of inbred strains indicates that environmental variance in exploratory behavior is due in nearly equal parts to shared and to nonshared environmental variance. Although nonshared environment is substantial, it is interesting that shared environmental experiences make mouse siblings similar in personality. This may be due to prenatal effects for siblings who lived in the womb at the same time or to shared environmental factors after birth, such as treatment by the mother mouse or by other sibling mice that increases sibling similarity. The relative importance of shared environmental effects might somehow be a function of the highly constrained environment of the laboratory, failing, for example, to provide the richness of the normal nonshared experiences of mouse pups. These findings, along with the control made possible by laboratory experimentation, suggest that systematic research on nonshared environment using inbred strains of mice would be fruitful, although no such research has yet been reported.

WHAT ARE THESE NONSHARED
ENVIRONMENTAL INFLUENCES?

The discovery of the importance of environmental experiences that are not shared is a finding of far-reaching significance for understanding the environmental contribution to development. It implies that the environment shared by children growing up in the same family does not make them similar to one another. Not only does this tell us that we have been barking up the wrong tree, it also points to the right tree. Instead of thinking about environmental influences on a family-by-family basis, we need to think on an individual-by-individual basis.

This requires a major shift in our views of how the family might affect children's development. For instance, we assume that factors that differ across families, such as socioeconomic status, parental education, and the marital relationship, are important. Yet this change in orientation tells us that, to the extent that these factors affect children growing up in the same family in a similar way, they cannot influence behavioral development. These factors may be important, but only if their impact is not experienced similarly by children in the family. This is such a revolutionary idea that it is difficult to grasp. Experiences shared by siblings cannot be important because if they were important they would make siblings similar. For example, if social class shared by siblings growing up in the same family is important for IQ, it would make siblings in the same family similar to one another even when siblings are genetically unrelated as in the case of adoptive siblings. In fact, this appears to be the case for IQ, but only in childhood. We know that in the long run such shared environmental factors are not important, because older siblings are not at all similar in IQ beyond the resemblance due to heredity. How else can we explain the fact that genetically unrelated siblings adopted into the same family early in life are not at all similar in IQ after childhood?

Because shared environment is of negligible importance and nearly all environmental variance is of the nonshared type, the critical question for development becomes: Why are children in the same family so different? The key to solving this puzzle is to study more than one child per family. Only by studying more than one child per family can we begin to explore different lives within the family and to identify those nonshared experiences that are critical in development. We can only understand how such apparently shared factors as socioeconomic status affect development by studying how, and why, siblings are influenced differently by them.

Three problems need to be tackled. First, in what ways do the experiences of siblings differ? Only differential experiences—not shared ones—can make a difference in their development. We need to document the nature and extent of experiences specific to each child within the family. Second, to what extent do such differential experiences affect siblings' developmental outcomes? That is, there may be differences in siblings' experiences that have no relation to their development. We need to study the relation between differential experiences and developmental outcomes.

The third problem is the thorny one of the interpretation of cause and effect. It cannot be assumed that a correlation between siblings' differential experiences and siblings' behavior means that the different experiences caused the behavior. It might be the other way around—that sibling differences in behavior lead to their different experiences. This is a notoriously intractable issue, but we do have some strategies for dealing with it. Longitudinal studies can help to unravel the threads of cause and effect by investigating whether one thing precedes the other. For example, suppose that differences in mothers' affection to siblings relate to children's self-esteem. It is possible that differential maternal affection causes changes in children's self-esteem, but it is also possible that mothers are differentially affectionate to their children on the basis of the children's self-esteem. That is, it might be easier to love children who feel good about themselves. Longitudinal data can indicate whether changes in maternal affection precede changes in children's self-esteem, which would suggest a causal direction from mother to child rather than the reverse. Twin and adoption studies can address the possibility that heredity is responsible for the association between differences in sibling experiences and developmental outcome. For example, twin data can pin down specific associations between nonshared environmental influences and developmental outcome of siblings. Because members of identical twin pairs do not differ genetically, we can relate behavioral differences within pairs of identical twins to differences in their experiences. If an association is found between child-specific (nonshared) experiences and differences within pairs of identical twins, such an association cannot be mediated genetically, but must be caused by nonshared environmental factors. This third problem is one that can be put off until we have identified the differential sibling experiences that are associated with developmental outcomes—problems 1 and 2.

In the chapters that follow, our focus will be on the sources of experiences within the family that are not shared: the origins of differences between siblings growing up in the same family. We draw both on biographical and autobiographical information and on the findings of systematic studies. The message is *not* that family experiences are unimportant: far from it. The message of this chapter is that the salient environmental features of development are those that are experienced differently by children growing up in the same family. These differential experiences of siblings include the experiences that derive from the different lives they lead in their family. The possible role of parents in creating different experiences for siblings is the topic of chapter 4. Chapter 5 examines the role of the siblings themselves in such differential experiences. Nonshared environment, of course, need not be limited to such differential experiences within the family. Family members lead different lives outside the family as well. Chapter 6 considers factors beyond the family, and chapter 7 broaches the possible role played by chance. Finally, in chapter 8 the implications of this new view of family influence for researchers, clinicians, and parents are discussed.

4

The Impact of Parents

"Her name is Gwen," said the grandmother. "Kiss her." I bent down and kissed the little goldy tuft. But she took no notice. She lay quite still with eyes shut. "Now go and kiss mother," said the grandmother. But mother did not want to kiss me. Very languid, leaning against some pillows, she was eating some sago.

—Katherine Mansfield, *Journal*

Katherine Mansfield writes here of the moment when she was taken to see her new baby sister, recalling a poignant instance of rejection by her mother. For Katherine, growing up in New Zealand in the 1890s in a family of five girls and a boy, the contrast between her parents' relationships with her extremely attractive sisters and her fat and homely self was painful. Her difficult relationship with her parents was exacerbated as, in resentment, she drew attention to herself with displays of temper, in marked contrast to her sisters' easy compliance. In a short story, "Juliet," she writes revealingly of her childhood, and describes herself as an ugly, moody, critical girl who was rejected by her family—the odd one out, the ugly duckling.

Glimpses of the early lives of writers show us that differences in their parents' behavior toward them and their siblings were often marked and painful, and that even when there were no extremes of partiality, the young children were often very conscious of differential treatment, affection, and interest. How general are such differences, and in what ways might they contribute to the differences in development of children growing up together? Although the issue of *differential* parental treatment extends beyond such preferences, we will begin with the parental partiality for particular siblings that looms so large in many writers' imaginative reflections on their early lives.

Three siblings, Edith, Osbert, and Sacheverell Sitwell, who grew up in an aristocratic family in England at the turn of the century and each became a remarkably talented poet or writer, have given us vivid and detailed accounts of their childhood. Edith's relationship with her mother differed greatly from those of her brothers. She felt herself to be completely rejected, writing of herself as "a changeling" and her parents as strangers. "I was unpopular with my parents from the moment of my birth," she wrote. Her socialite mother's neglect and insensitivity towards her are a repeated theme in her writings; she gives a horrifying, if vindictive, portrait of an unloving, egotistical, cruel parent, leading a vapid, useless life. "Her rages were the only reality in her life."

Edith's brothers saw their mother very differently. Osbert, the loved son born five years after Edith, writes of his mother's "unusual beauty and strange temperament, her kindness, indulgence. . . . I was in the happy position as a small child of being my mother's favourite. I played on her bed, and upset everything with impunity. I adored her." To the third child, Sacheverell, his mother was also a figure of affection, beauty, and romance. Victoria Glendinning in her illuminating biography of Edith points to accounts by the three siblings of the very same incidents, seen very differently.

WHAT DO SIBLINGS SAY?

The Sitwells were an extraordinary family in their exceptional talents, their circumstances, and in the eccentricities and extreme behavior of their parents. Yet the theme of marked difference in parents' behavior to different children within the same family is far from exceptional. It recurs insistently in the biographies and the autobiographies of writers. The preference of parents for one or another of their children has often been distinguished by biographers as important in fostering the intellectual development and personality of writers: the motivation to break from the family world to a larger culture, the restless search for love and appreciation, the insecurity of their relationships. In the case of Mary Wollstonecraft, the pioneer feminist who published her manifesto *A Vindication of the Rights of Woman* in 1792, the case is surely a powerful one. Biographer Clare Tomalin argues convincingly for the importance of Mary's continuing sense of the disparity in affection and attention given to her and her brother in her development as a champion of women's rights:

> A sense of grievance may have been her most important endowment. . . . The overt preference given to Ned [her older brother] in terms of love and money stung her quite as sharply as any of the injustices of her life. . . . From a very early age she nourished the sense that she was unappreciated and denied affection that was her due.

This theme is also revealed in systematic studies of children and their parents. In the 1950s in one of the first major studies of siblings, Helen Koch interviewed a large number of 5- and 6-year-olds, and included questions about how their parents had behaved toward them and their siblings. The children's replies show clearly how salient the issue of differential treatment was to them, especially to the firstborn children. Two-thirds of the 360 children interviewed reported that their mother either favored them or their sibling, and only one-third described more equitable treatment. The firstborn, especially, did not feel championed by their mothers and spoke out clearly about the inequities they perceived in their parents' behavior toward them. The life of their younger sibling had real appeal to many:

"Yes, I would like to change places with my baby brother. Then I could yell my head off and my mamma would take care of nobody but me." "People are on her side." "She gets more attention."

But most children, whether first- or laterborn, also mentioned being favored in some way:

"I can do dangerous things that my brother can't do." "I don't have to eat spinach." "If I cry for things, mother says let me have them." "I can hit her but she can't hit me." "Sometimes I take things from my brother. Mother says give it to me."

In the families in which Koch interviewed both siblings, it is notable that the children did not agree about their parents' alignment. Their disagreement was particularly marked about their father's alignment: siblings disagreed twice as often as they agreed about their father's partiality. Among very young siblings, overt jealousy of the other child's relationship with the father is often more marked than jealousy of the sibling-mother relationship. Possibly it is this more intense emotional reaction of children to their sibling's relationship with their father that is linked to wider discrepancies in siblings' perceptions of differential treatment. If children feel especially sensitive to the affection that their sibling receives from their father, signs of that affection may have particular salience; they may loom especially large for the jealous child, and appear less significant for the child who is confident of a father's affection.

Interviews with older children—adolescents, and siblings in middle childhood—tell a similar story. Clear differences in siblings' perceptions of their parents' relationships with them were found for example in a major study of a nationally representative sample of 1,077 U.S. families. From this sample, 348 families with two siblings aged between 11 and 17 were interviewed, with each sibling and parent questioned individually about parental rules, expectations about chores, closeness to mother and father, and the extent to which the children were given a say in family decisions. The sibling pairs described considerable differences, especially in maternal closeness and in the extent to which the children had a say in decisions. Four other studies of adolescents and young adults asked siblings to report directly on the extent to which their parents treated them similarly or differently, using a questionnaire called the Sibling Inventory of Differential Experience (SIDE), which asks respondents to compare themselves to their sibling regarding treatment by their mother and by their father. Nearly half of the siblings reported differences.

To make the results of this research more meaningful, you may wish to consider your view of your parents' differential interactions with you and your sibling. Table 4.1 contains the SIDE items relevant to mothers' and fathers' treatment, as well as scoring instructions and comparison data for a large sample of siblings.

Do these differences in siblings' perceptions of parental treatment merely reflect parents' different responses to ge-

Table 4.1   Sibling Inventory of Differential Experience (SIDE)
Parental Interactions with You and Your Sibling

This questionnaire is designed to ask how similarly your mother and father treated you and your sibling. Compare yourself to your sibling (or one of your siblings) when you were growing up and living at home. If your parents were divorced or if one died, answer the questions for the mother and father with whom you lived for the longest period of time. Scoring instructions and comparison scores are provided at the end of the questionnaire.

1 = In general, this parent has been much more this way toward my sibling than me.

2 = In general, this parent has been a bit more this way toward my sibling than me.

3 = In general, this parent has been the same toward my sibling and me.

4 = In general, this parent has been a bit more this way toward me than my sibling.

5 = In general, this parent has been much more this way toward me than my sibling.

	Toward Sibling Much More		Same		Toward Me Much More
Mother:					
1) Has been strict with us.	1	2	3	4	5
2) Has been proud of the things we have done.	1	2	3	4	5
3) Has enjoyed doing things with us.	1	2	3	4	5
4) Has been sensitive to what we think and feel.	1	2	3	4	5

Table 4.1 *(Continued)*

	Toward Sibling Much More		Same		Toward Me Much More
5) Has punished us for our misbehavior.	1	2	3	4	5
6) Has shown interest in the things we like to do.	1	2	3	4	5
7) Has blamed us for what another family member did.	1	2	3	4	5
8) Has tended to favor one of us.	1	2	3	4	5
9) Has disciplined us.	1	2	3	4	5

	Toward Sibling Much More		Same		Toward Me Much More
Father					
1) Has been strict with us.	1	2	3	4	5
2) Has been proud of the things we have done.	1	2	3	4	5
3) Has enjoyed doing things with us.	1	2	3	4	5
4) Has been sensitive to what we think and feel.	1	2	3	4	5
5) Has punished us for our misbehavior.	1	2	3	4	5
6) Has shown interest in the things we like to do.	1	2	3	4	5

Table 4.1 *(Continued)*

	Toward Sibling Much More		Same		Toward Me Much More
7) Has blamed us for what another family member did.	1	2	3	4	5
8) Has tended to favor one of us.	1	2	3	4	5
9) Has disciplined us.	1	2	3	4	5

Scoring: Separately for the mother and father items, add your answers for items 2, 3, 4, 6, and 8 and divide by 5 to create an affection score. A control score is obtained by adding items 1, 5, 7, and 9 and dividing by 4. For both scales for mothers and fathers, young adult siblings yield an average score of 3.0. The extent to which your affection and control scores are below or above 3.0 indicates how differentially you view your parents' treatment of you and your sibling.

netic differences between the siblings? That is, are genetic differences between the siblings responsible for differential parental affection, for example? A twin study and an adoption study, both using the SIDE, addressed this issue but yielded conflicting results. Identical twins reported less differential treatment by their parents than fraternal twins in parental affection and especially in parental control. This finding suggests the possibility that genetic factors affect siblings' perceptions of differential parental treatment, although it is also possible that parental treatment of identical twins, who are difficult to distinguish physically, might not be comparable to other siblings. This latter hypothesis is strengthened by SIDE comparisons between biological and adoptive siblings. Adoptive siblings, who are not similar genetically, are treated no more differently by their parents than are bio-logical siblings.

WHAT DO SIBLINGS DO?

Children's sensitivity to differential parental behavior is evi-dent not only in their comments on the pattern of family relationships; it is revealed to us in their actions. In a series of studies in Cambridge, England, using naturalistic observations with as little interference as possible in families' daily interac-tion, we found that extremely early in childhood children re-spond immediately and directly to their parents' interaction with their siblings. These studies include a longitudinal study of firstborn children followed from before the birth of their sibling through the infancy of the secondborn, and two further studies that focus on secondborn children followed from their second until their sixth year.

Several lines of evidence from these observations demon-strate the unquestionable salience to young children of the relationship that their siblings have with the parents. Observa-tions made during the months after the birth of a sibling showed that in many families the interaction between mother and baby had a marked effect on the behavior of the first child; some of the firstborn children responded to a high propor-tion—as high as three out of four—of the interactions between their mothers and baby siblings. The most common response was a protest or a demand for precisely the same attention that the sibling was getting, as the following examples illustrate. In the first incident, from the study of firstborn children followed through the birth and infancy of their sibling, 14-month-old

Malcolm was playing with his mother, watched vigilantly by 3-year-old Virginia:

> Mother to Malcolm (playing with Lego): I'll make you a little car, Malcolm.
> Virginia: Well, I want one.
> Mother to Malcolm: Shall I make you a car? Mmm?
> Virginia: Don't let him have the red pieces.
> Mother to Malcolm (picking him up and imitating his noises): Wawwaw! Wawwaw!
> Virginia: Can I sit beside you? Can I sit on knee?
> Mother to Virginia: Is that just because Malcolm's up here?
> Virginia: Yes.
> Mother to Virginia: Come on then.

A common response of the firstborn children to the interaction of their mothers and siblings was to "mirror" the action of the baby that had drawn the mother's attention, as in the next incident. Alistair, aged 35 months, watched intently when his mother exclaimed playfully at his younger sister Shirley's muddy hands:

> Mother to Shirley: Hullo Shirley, what's that? Guess! Mud! Look at you! Poofy! Dirty.

Alistair promptly ran to the flower bed and covered his hands with mud, then ran to his mother to show her his dirty hands.

Several children in the study also copied their younger siblings' "naughty" actions, if these drew attention from the mother, as in the following incident between 3-year-old Duncan and his 14-month-old brother Robbie, who was pulling papers and magazines out of the bookcase:

Mother to Robbie: No! Stop!
Duncan immediately runs over and starts pulling out papers
too, looking at his mother.
Mother to Duncan: No Duncan, there's no need for you! You
know better—or don't you?
Duncan: No!

The ways in which the older siblings responded varied, depend-
ing in part upon the nature of the interaction between the
mother and sibling. Sometimes they tried to join the play
between mother and baby, sometimes they attempted to disrupt it or to draw attention to themselves—often with unfortunate results, since they frequently chose to do exactly what
annoyed their mothers most. Sometimes they simply broke
down in misery. The significance to them of the happy play
between their mother and baby sibling was all too poignantly
clear. The response of the firstborn depended very much on
their temperament, too. One little girl, Sally, found changes in
routine or unexpected events very difficult to take—she was
extreme on the temperamental trait of "adaptability" in the
psychologists' terms. She was also emotionally intense, and she
reacted with particularly intense protests when her mother
became involved with her sister Ruby:

Mother to Ruby (commenting on her playing): Are you enjoying yourself, Ruby?
Sally (shouting crossly): She can't have that any more!

In contrast, Susan, an even-tempered, easy-going, adaptable
girl would join in happily when her mother started to play with
her younger brother Alan, as in this incident:

Alan is engaged in "running away" from his mother (crawling
fast, with an excited noise):

Mother to Alan: Bye-bye! Bye-bye!
Susan (joins in by chasing Alan, to his great excitement): I
going to catch him! I am! I am!

Was this sensitivity to their mothers' behavior with the new
arrival simply a *firstborn* phenomenon—one facet of the response to displacement that is so common after the birth of a
second child? Would such close attention to the relationship
between mother and firstborn be shown by a laterborn child?
In two studies of families with preschool children we focused
on the secondborn children, and we found that children as
young as 14 months were vigilant monitors of their mothers'
relationship with their older siblings. They were particularly
attentive to any interaction in which emotions were expressed;
playful excited games or disputes between mother and older
sibling were of special interest. Again, individual differences in
the type of response were marked, but rarely were emotional
exchanges between mother and firstborn ignored: only 12 percent went unattended.

The children's responses to disputes were particularly interesting: sometimes they attempted to support one or other of
the antagonists, and their responses showed they understood
quite a bit about what the disputants wanted, and that they
made evaluative judgments very early on about their older
siblings' behavior. The little girl Nan in the next example is
only 24 months old, but joins the argument between her
mother and older sibling Clare with a judgmental comment:

Clare aged five shows her mother that she has drawn on a piece
of jigsaw puzzle:
Mother to Clare: You aren't supposed to draw on them Clare.
You should know better. You only draw on pieces of paper. You
don't draw on puzzles.

Clare to Mother (crossly): Why?
Mother to Clare: Because they aren't pieces of paper.
Nan: Naughty!
Mother: Yes that is a naughty thing to do.

Judgment was passed on an older sister in the next example also, this time by 26-month-old Polly:

Mother and Helen are arguing over whether TV should be turned off:
Mother to Helen: Switch it off.
Helen to Mother: I don't want you to switch it off! No! (repeated 8 times).
Polly to Helen: No!
Helen to Mother: No! (repeated 5 times). Naughty Mummy!
Mother to Helen: Hey! Come on.
Helen to Mother: No (repeated 3 times).
Polly to Helen (holding her mother): Not naughty. Naughty Helen (hits Helen).

A third and very different analysis—this time a study of children's conversational abilities—told the same story. Much of the talk in a family is not addressed to the younger children; it is an important—but rarely studied—developmental advance when children become able to join these larger family conversations. To document the growth of this ability we studied children's interventions in the talk between other family members: their attempts to join, interrupt, or contribute to the conversation between other family members.

We discovered that children monitor closely the conversation between their mothers and their siblings, and interrupt such conversation to draw attention to themselves with increasing effectiveness and, indeed, skill. Early in a child's third year, these interventions are usually straightforwardly self-centered, even when they are focused on the topic of the conversation they are interrupting. One of the children we observed commented to his mother, when she enquired what he was doing, "I am drawing a bus." His 26-month-old younger brother intervened to say, "I don't like it." By 36 months of age the children managed on a high proportion of occasions to turn the mother-and-sibling discourse to the topic that they were most interested in—themselves! In one incident, 5-year-old Christy was playing a pretend shopping game with her mother as customer. Anny, her younger sister, intervened in a successful move that drew her mother to play with *her:*

> Mother has asked Christy (as shopkeeper) for bananas.
> Christy to Mother: I don't have any bananas today.
> Mother to Christy: Oh dear and I wanted to buy some!
> Anny to Mother: In my shop there *is* bananas! You buy my bananas now!
> Mother to Anny: OK! (laughs)

Our observations show that very early in childhood children promptly and insistently react to the interactions between their siblings and their parents. The interviews with the siblings show us that the children perceive differences in how they are treated and frequently mind very much about those differences. The responses of Mary Wollstonecraft and Katherine Mansfield are, it appears, far from unusual in this respect.

WHAT DO PARENTS SAY?

How do *parents* perceive their own behavior toward their different children? Running through the letters and diaries of the families of our writers is evidence from parents of the differences in their relationships with their children. Henry James, for instance, came to be his mother's favorite son. According to the biographer Leon Edel, Mary James showed her preference for Henry quite openly. When, as young adults both sons were intermittently ill, she fussed over Henry's illness, but

> treated William as a self-centered hypochondriac. Her letters make quite free with his condition; he complains too much; he has a "morbid sympathy" with every form of physical trouble; he worries excessively; "He must express every fluctuation of feeling."

Shortly before his death, Henry the father wrote to Henry the son: "I can't help feeling that you are the one that has cost us the least trouble, and given us always the most delight. Especially do I mind mother's perfect joy in you the last few months of her life, and your perfect sweetness to her."

What is the picture from parents today? In separate studies in Colorado in the United States and Cambridge, England, mothers of young siblings were asked directly about the quality of their relationships with their different children and the extent to which they treat the siblings differently. Despite strong social norms that parents should treat siblings similarly, only a third of mothers in the Colorado sample reported feeling a similar intensity and extent of affection for both of their children, and only a third said that they give similar attention to both. In most of these families, the younger children receive more affection and attention, according to their mothers. In each study, only 12 percent reported finding discipline equally easy or difficult with their two children, and only 12 percent said that they disciplined their children with equal frequency. The extent of similarity of the results from the two studies is interesting, given other differences between the families. For instance, in the Colorado study, 52 percent of mothers reported feeling more affectionate toward their younger child (on average four years old) than to their older, and only 13 percent said that they felt more affection toward their older child; in the Cambridge study, where the younger sibling averaged six and a half years, the equivalent figures were 61 percent and 10 percent.

SHOULD WE TAKE INTERVIEWS SERIOUSLY?

To live over other people's lives is nothing unless we live over their perceptions, live over the growth, the change, the varying intensity of the same—since it was by these things they themselves lived.
—Henry James

The evidence from interviews in the studies of early and middle childhood tells us clearly that both young children and their parents see considerable differences in their behavior to siblings growing up together. But what weight should we place on such interview reports—whether from children or their parents? Clearly the children's perceptions are of importance—possibly more significant than any outsider's account of the matter, however skillful an observer of the family he or she may be (recall Emma's admonition to Mr. Knightly quoted in chapter 1). How children feel about themselves as they grow up, how they approach the world outside the family and deal with the inevitable frustrations and problems, may very well be more clearly linked to how they *feel* they have been loved, appreciated, and valued in earlier years than to how an outsider would describe their family relationships. Parents' accounts of differences in their behavior to their children assume greater significance because they go against the socially desired response that siblings be treated the same.

Social pressure obviously looms larger in interviews with adults than with children. How seriously, then, can we take the mothers' accounts? Three general points are worth bearing in mind. First, the mothers in each study were very familiar with their interviewers, and were relaxed and at ease, indeed friendly with their interviewers. Second, and no doubt related, they appeared to have no hesitation about describing socially unacceptable features of their relationships with their children. Consider, for example, the comments from three different mothers about their reactions to their firstborn children in the months after the birth of the second, when the mothers were tired and stressed: "I feel like murdering her. I dread the sound of her feet along the corridor." "I've got so I can't stand her. She has me in tears every day. It's bad really." "I was very miserable. I smacked Sue all the time. I was screaming and shouting at her. *He's* very easy in the day. Very undemanding. If he'd been like her, I'd be in hospital." Such extreme desperation was, fortunately, not very common. Nor was it exclusively focused upon firstborn children or found only in the immediate postpartum period. A mother who was very much at ease with her first child describes her feelings about her second child:

"When she was about 6 months, daily I felt over the top. I stayed in bed because I felt I might hit her."

The third point to keep in mind regarding the validity of these interviews with mothers is perhaps the most important: there was some agreement between what the mothers *said* about their behavior to their two children and what we *saw*, just as there was agreement between some aspects of what they said about the siblings' behavior toward each other and what we observed. We turn next to our observations of the parents' behavior.

TO WHAT EXTENT DO PARENTS BEHAVE DIFFERENTIALLY TO THEIR CHILDREN?

Mothers who are at home with a toddler or preschool-aged child and a relatively sophisticated 5-, 6-, or 7-year-old behave quite differently toward those two children. Whether the evidence comes from unconstrained naturalistic studies of families in which the mothers are carrying out their usual household jobs—washing the dishes, cleaning, or gardening—or from more "structured" situations in which they are asked to play games with their children in front of the videocamera, the story is similar. Differences in attention to the two children are most marked, followed by differences in control and in affection.

It is not a surprising finding, given the children's differences in developmental stage. As Sandra Scarr put it, "Can you imagine speaking to a 1-year-old as you would to a 2-year-old, even if you were the most insensitive person in the world?" We must also consider parents' behavior in relation to their children's experiences at *particular and comparable ages*. Did each child have comparable experiences of affectionate attention and love from mother during infancy or early childhood, for example? The Colorado study gives us evidence on this issue, because we were able to study each sibling as an individual at the ages of 12, 24, and 36 months playing and talking with his or her mother.

What we found was, initially, rather a surprise. We had expected to see considerable differences in a mother's behavior to her successive children when the same age, but we discovered, to the contrary, that mothers were quite consistent to their two children at the same age, though they did not behave consistently to the same child over time. That is, a mother who was particularly affectionate and responsive to her 12-month-old was not, relative to the other mothers, particularly affectionate to that same child a year later; but she was relatively affectionate to a subsequent child when the child reached 12 months. Thus the children's particular stage of development has a surprisingly profound effect on their mothers' behavior, at least in the circumstances in which we were studying them.

Key for our interest in differential behavior is one implication of these results: at any one time point, the siblings in a family *are* at different ages and at different developmental stages. Again, the evidence has shown us that a mother behaves very differently—even to the *same* child—according to his or her developmental stage. To put it concretely, consider a family in which the mother is particularly affectionate to both her children as 12-month-olds, but not especially affectionate to them as 36-month-olds. A child at this later stage, receiving relatively little affection, will daily be witness to the particular affection the mother shows the 12-month-old sibling.

The evidence for *consistency* toward siblings when they are the same age has an important implication for the puzzle of why siblings develop so differently. It suggests that although two children have had rather similar experiences with their mother when they were similar ages throughout early childhood, these experiences of direct interaction with the mother do not per se contribute to the children's different developmental outcome. Witnessing *differential* behavior to self and to other children may be more important than similar experiences of *direct* interaction with the parents. Seeing your mother's evident affection for your sibling may override any amount of affection you in fact receive. This is an idea directly at odds with the usual view of what matters in parenting—an idea that collides with current psychological theory, but is definitely worth pursuing.

The usual view is that it is the direct impact of how a parent relates to a child that influences that child's development. We argue that children are sensitive not only to how their parents relate to them, but also to how their parents relate to their siblings, and that children monitor and respond to that other relationship just as they monitor the relationship between their parents. This is a shift from viewing the child as child-of-the-parent to child-as-family-member.

Do these differences in mothers' behavior matter for children's development? Is there any empirical evidence that the outcomes of individual children are linked to differential experiences with their parents?

LINKS TO OUTCOME

The salience of perceived differences in parental treatment is most vividly brought home to us by the autobiographical and fictional explorations of patterns of parental interest and affection. For Charles Dickens, for example, one of the worst moments in a stressful childhood that involved repeated hardship and poverty was an incident of *relative* deprivation, when he was faced with the contrast between his situation and that of his older sister Fanny. While he was sent to work in a factory just two days after he was twelve, she won a scholarship to the Royal Academy of Music. He was profoundly hurt by the contrast between his own disregarded condition and the parental pride at her success. He recalled being taken to see Princess Augusta preside at a prize day at the Royal Academy, at which Fanny received a silver medal:

> I could not bear to think of myself—beyond the reach of all such honorable emulation and success. . . . The tears ran down my face. . . . I prayed, when I went to bed that night, to be lifted out of the humiliation and neglect in which I was. I never had suffered so much before.

Dickens's sense of the importance of children's perceptions of injustice and inequities in their experiences was acute, as a comment in *Great Expectations* makes clear:

> In the little world in which children have their existence, whosoever brings them up, there is nothing so finely perceived and so finely felt, as injustice.

From the very first investigations of this question, differential experiences with parents appear to show links with children's outcomes. The study of a national sample of adolescent siblings mentioned earlier showed that differential parental treatment (as rated by both the parents and the siblings) relates to sibling differences in adjustment and delinquency. Specifically, both parental and sibling reports indicate that the sibling who has been closest to the mother, who has had more say in family decision making, and has had higher parental chore expectations, as compared to the other siblings, is better adjusted psychologically. Similar results were found in a recent twin study, although another sibling study found that differential parental treatment was not much related to sibling differences in personality. Adjustment, which seems to be the prime target of differential parental treatment, was not assessed in this latter study.

Associations between differential parental treatment and outcome are not limited to interview and self-report data. The emotional adjustment of the firstborn children participating in the Colorado study was studied when they were 7 years old, and its relation to their experience of differential treatment from their mothers (assessed both through maternal report and by observation) was examined. The results showed that differential maternal affection and control were linked to children's worrying, anxiety, and depression. Children who experienced more maternal control or less affection than their siblings were more likely to be anxious or depressive. Differential maternal behavior was also associated with children's antisocial behavior (disobedience, teasing, argumentative and hyperactive behavior); in families in which the mother controlled the older much more than the younger sibling, the older child was likely to show relatively high levels of problem behavior. It could also be that the mothers were attempting to exert control over the older siblings in these

81

families *because* they were so difficult. We will consider the question of cause and effect next.

PARENTAL DIFFERENTIATION AS A RESPONSE TO DIFFERENCES BETWEEN SIBLINGS

The question of how far the differences in parental behavior are responses to differences in the children's personality and behavior toward others is a key one.

What we ultimately want to explain is the difference in the siblings' developmental outcome. If the differences in parental behavior are simply responses to preexisting differences in children's personalities or intelligence, and these characteristics of the children show a clear relation to the later adjustment differences, then it is of course possible that the differences in parental behavior do not make an independent contribution to the differences in adjustment. In other words, the parents could be simply responding to stable differences between the siblings that show continuity over time. If so, it is possible that connections between parental differentiation and differences in the children's developmental outcome are not causal, but both reflect the continuing personality differences. Is there any evidence that differential parental behavior is independently associated with adjustment outcomes of children?

The answer, from the studies so far, is yes. When researchers analyze their results so as to take account of differences in siblings' personalities, the differences in parental treatment are found to make an independent, additional contribution to the differences in child adjustment. Take the case of differences between siblings in their sense of self-worth and their perception of how socially competent they are. The sense of self-competence and self-worth is centrally important in children's emotional development. Differences in perceived self-competence during middle childhood show links to later depressive feelings: children who feel they are disliked by their peers and inadequate in their social relations are more likely to report being depressed when they get older. So it is important that we should understand what leads to feelings of self-competence. It is often suggested that early experiences—especially those within the relationship with the mother—are significant here. But there has been very little direct study of early family influences on such feelings. In a recent follow-up of one of our Cambridge studies, the siblings each assessed their self-competence when they were on average 6 and 9 years old. We found no relationship between the siblings' sense of self-competence and self-worth—another example of sibling differences.

When we examined what features of family experience related to the marked differences in perceived self-competence, we found that differential maternal and paternal behavior, both at the time the children were assessed and at earlier observations, correlated with the children's feelings about themselves. Most important, this contribution to the variance in the siblings' sense of self-worth was independent of earlier differences in the children's personalities.

We used statistical techniques to investigate the issue of whether the variation between individual children in their sense of self-worth is explained primarily by earlier differences in their personality or whether other factors, such as differential parental behavior, add to the variation. Analysis showed that in the case of the Cambridge siblings, after the variation

83

in self-worth that is related to earlier assessed personality differences is taken into account, differences in parents' behavior to their two children added to our ability to explain the remaining differences in sense of self-worth. Children whose mothers had shown relatively more affection to siblings had a lower sense of self-competence and self-worth than children whose mothers had shown them relatively more affection. This effect held up for the sample of Cambridge children even after we had taken account of the variance in self-worth that was linked to earlier personality differences between the children.

Other important features of the network of family relationships also contributed to the children's feelings of self-worth, as we will see in the next chapter, but the significance of parental differential behavior stood out. Although we should be cautious about inferring cause from these correlations, this evidence does suggest that differences in parent behavior do matter in terms of children's developmental outcome, at least in this important domain.

Another relevant research finding from a new study of differential experiences and adjustment of identical twins provides evidence that genetic factors are not responsible for the association. Correlating differential treatment of identical twins with their personality differences constitutes a rigorous test of nonshared environmental influence. Because identical twins are identical genetically, such associations cannot be brought about by genetic factors. The test gains in rigor because it is likely that identical twins share environmental influences to a greater extent than non-twin siblings. Nonetheless, identical twins' reports of their parents' differential treatment were found to be linked to differences in depression and sense of well-being in the twins: to the extent that parents treated the identical twins differently, the twins differed.

THE IMPACT OF PARENTS

A Word on Birth Order

When differences in parents' behavior to their different children are discussed, often the first issue that comes to mind is the birth order of the children. It is frequently assumed that parents systematically treat their firstborn child differently from laterborn children. The common belief is that parents are more anxious and less competent with their firstborn, especially when the children are infants. In fact, the evidence for such systematic birth order differences is not good. In both our Colorado and our Cambridge studies, for example, there were no systematic differences in mothers' behavior to their first and secondborn children when they were seen at the same age. But even if there was more impressive evidence for birth order effects in parental behavior, how relevant would it be for our arguments?

In an important sense such differences are not relevant. This is because individual differences in personality and psychopathology in the general population—the differences in outcome that we are trying to explain—are *not* clearly linked to the birth order of the individuals. Although this evidence goes against many widely held and cherished beliefs, the judgment of those who have looked carefully at a large number of studies is that birth order plays only a bit-part in the drama of sibling differences. The special achievements and eminence of firstborn individuals that are so often referred to disappear when factors such as the education and social circumstances of families, and their links to family size, are taken into account. If there are no systematic differences in personality according to birth order, then any differences in parental behavior that are associated with birth order cannot be very significant for later developmental outcome.

85

With these first studies of differential parent-child relationships, the initial steps are being taken toward clarifying the
significance these discrepant experiences may have for children's development. Many questions remain to be answered,
prominent among them the issue of how important are perceptions of discrepancies. In both the autobiographical material
and the interviews, we draw on individuals' perceptions of what
happened within their family. It is an empirical question
whether these perceptions of parental relationships matter
more than directly observable features of parents' behavior
with their children. These perceptions may, of course, be
closely linked to what is observed by others. Many psychologists tend to dismiss the perceptions of family members in
favor of what they—the psychologists—can "see," but as yet
we know little about the agreement between the two sources
of information about family relationships.

A second question concerns the *nature* of the differential
behavior that is important. When a mother turns from attempting to control a trying, argumentative child to play with
a delightful sibling, there are likely to be differences in the
warmth and affection expressed in her voice and manner,
differences in the content of what she says (critical and controlling to one, amusedly affectionate to the other), and differences in the attention that she gives to the two of them.
Any or all of these differences may be noticed and responded
to. Any or all of them may turn out to be related to later
developmental differences. In all likelihood there will be
changes over time—as the siblings grow up—in which aspects are significant. Nor should we think of differential parental relationships as being limited to childhood. Studies of
elderly parents of adult children often document marked
preferences. Joan Aldous and her colleagues argue in their

study of elderly parents that such differential behavior increases over the life span:

> Parents do differentiate among their children. Just as changing times and differences among children modify parents' conformity to the norm of equal children, so do children's characteristics and life events weaken parents' allegiance to the norm of equal attachment.

And finally, that intractable question of cause and effect, including the contribution of personality differences between siblings to the parental differentiation, looms large. Longitudinal studies will be essential to clarifying the patterns of influence, as will behavioral genetic studies that disentangle genetic contributions to these associations. Similar issues must be faced in a second major potential source of different experiences within the family—the sibling relationship itself. This is the topic of the next chapter.

5

Sibling Influences

Well, he's nice to me. And he sneaks into my bed at night time from Mummy. I think I'd be very lonely without Carl. I play with him a lot and he thinks up lots of ideas and it's very exciting. He comes and meets me at the gate after school and I think that's very friendly. . . . He's very kind. . . . Don't really know what I'd do without a brother.

—Nancy, 10 years old, talks about her 6-year-old brother Carl

She's pretty disgusting and we don't talk to each other much. I don't really know much about her. [Interviewer: What is it you particularly like about her?] Nothing. Sometimes when I do something wrong she tells me off quite cruelly.

—Carl talks about Nancy

No one would doubt that the relationship between a mother and her child is experienced differently by each of the two. Nor would we assume that what a father feels about his child is very similar to what his child feels about him, however deep the affection between them. Psychologists who study parents and their children have thought hard about the separate contribution and experience of each partner in the relationship and how these contributions change as children grow up. They may talk about "the parent-child relationship" as if the bond was a unitary one, implying that its particular qualities of warmth or conflict were the same for both members of the dyad, but they also focus on the differences in what parent and child experience. So, too, we recognize that within a marriage the two partners may experience very different feelings, may see what is happening within the marriage quite differently and describe the quality of that dyadic relationship very differently. There can be "two marriages," to borrow Jessie Bernard's phrase.

In contrast, psychologists usually approach the study of siblings as if both partners were affected similarly by the relationship. They have dissected with care different dimensions of the relationship—showing that conflict, affection, and control are relatively independent, for instance, and that some pairs can quarrel and argue ceaselessly yet also show much friendliness. The extent of conflict between two siblings is not closely related to the affection, cooperation, and support that they show for one another. But the question of whether there are differences in the experiences of siblings in the same relationship has not been explored systematically: it simply has not been a matter of interest to psychologists, who have been more concerned with painting the quality of the relationship in broad brush strokes and with exploring its links with other family relationships.

For our central topic—the issue of why siblings grow up to be so different from one another—the question is clearly relevant. The possibility that different experiences within the sibling relationship contribute to the differences in individual outcomes must be taken seriously. Nancy and Carl, the siblings from a Cambridge study with whom we began this chapter, talk about their relationship in very different ways, and they are not unusual. A moment's reflection about families that we know well or on the accounts in autobiographical and biographical writing shows how differently the relationship between a pair of siblings can be experienced. Most notable are differences in affectionate interest and in control or dominance—the latter usually but not inevitably linked to birth order, at least in childhood. But the differences in outcome that we have to explain are not simply birth order differences. Are there important differences in the relationship between siblings, that are independent of birth order, which could contribute to these outcome differences?

Autobiographical and biographical materials show repeatedly that there can be notable differences in the affection, the admiration and interest, the jealousy, the irritation and antagonism, and the concern that brothers and sisters show for each other that are not straightforwardly linked to birth order. Some of the incidents that we have already considered make this point: Charles Dickens's reaction to his sister Fanny's success, and the difference between Mark Twain's (Tom Sawyer's) behavior to his brother and Henry's (Sid's) attitude to him, for instance. A particularly poignant example is given to us in George Eliot's accounts of her childhood relationship with her brother Isaac—both in her poem "Brother and Sister" and in her portrayal of Maggie and Tom Tulliver in *The Mill on the Floss*. Maggie, the adoring, worshipping younger sister, is a picture drawn directly from her creator's experiences with Isaac. The lyrical account of the early closeness between the young siblings and the older brother's gradual loss of interest in his sister brings the differences in the two children's experiences within the relationship and the sister's suffering at the disparity in affectionate interest movingly to our attention. The description in *The Mill on the Floss* of Tom/Isaac's return from school for the first time captures the beginnings of this loss and the differences in the two children's feelings for the other. Note that Yap the dog receives as much attention as poor Maggie:

> Mrs. Tulliver stood with her arms open; Maggie jumped first on one leg and then on the other; while Tom descended from the gig, and said, with a masculine reticence as to the tender emotions, "Hallo! Yap—what! Are you there?"
> Nevertheless he submitted to be kissed willingly enough, while his blue-grey eyes wandered towards the croft and the lambs and the river, where he promised himself that he would begin to fish the first thing tomorrow morning.

In real life, when Isaac was given a pony of his own, as the biographer Gordon Haight notes, "riding absorbed him completely, and he found no time to play with the disconsolate Mary Anne." Her daydreams of what she longed for—his attention and love—are spelled out in this passage (not included in the final version of the book) which tells how Maggie

> down by the holly made her little world just like she would like it to be. . . . Tom never went to school, and liked no one to play with him but Maggie; they went out together somewhere everyday, and carried either hot buttered cakes with them because it was baking day, or apple puffs well sugared; Tom was never angry with her for forgetting things, and liked her to tell him tales. . . . Above all, Tom loved her—oh, so much,—more, even than she loved him, so that he would always want to have her with him and be afraid of vexing her; and he as well as everyone else, thought her very clever.

Mary Anne's pain as her brother's interest in her waned was not paralleled in Isaac's experience. Growing up with a sibling meant strikingly different things to Isaac/Tom and Mary

Anne/Maggie (George Eliot), as it did, evidently, to Mark Twain and his brother Henry (Tom Sawyer and Sid), and to Henry and William James.

DIFFERENCES IN DOMINANCE AND CONTROL

It was the difference in affectionate interest and admiration between George Eliot and her brother that was so poignant, but disparities within the sibling relationship arise, as we will see, in a range of dimensions—the most obvious discrepancies being in the leadership, dominance, control, and teaching exercised by each child. Differences in the dominance of siblings in games are vivid in the accounts of writers' childhoods. Recall Shelley's hair-raising experiments with electricity—his delight and his sister Hellen's terror at the exploits that he organized (see chapter 1). For Leo Tolstoy, his brother Nicholas was always the leader and mentor in the childhood games. Laurence Housman writes of his brother Alfred's "training" of the younger siblings, such as the games in which he taught them the movements of the planets. Each took the part of a planet and moved appropriately around the others on the lawn:

> I was the sun, my brother Basil the earth, Alfred was the moon. My part in the game was to stay where I was and rotate on my own axis; Basil's was to go round me in a wide circle rotating as he went; Alfred, performing the movements of the moon, skipped round him without rotation. And that is how I learned, and have ever since remembered, the primary relations of the sun, the earth, and the moon.

Such dominance shaded, in some families, into bullying—at least as perceived by the younger sibling. Aggressive dominance by one sibling could be described (with surprising charity) as simply the accepted mode of teaching, as in Anthony Trollope's account of his treatment at his older brother's hands:

> There have been hot words between us, for perfect friendship bears and allows hot words. But in those school days he was, of all my foes, the worst. In accordance with the practice of the College, which submits or did then submit, much of the tuition of the younger boys to the elder, he was my tutor; and in his capacity of teacher and ruler, he had studied the theories of Draco. . . . The result was, as part of his daily exercise, he thrashed me with a big stick.

Acid criticism and effortless superiority on the part of the older sibling, and the mismatch of their abilities profoundly colored some sibling relationships, as the autobiographical writing of Henry James makes clear. As Leon Edel, his biographer, shows, William "aggressively rejected" his brother in a series of incidents involving merciless lampooning and criticism.

Other older siblings took their responsibility for the intellectual nurturance and education as well as the emotional support of their younger siblings very seriously—and more kindly. The letters of Anton Chekhov and of John Keats to their respective younger siblings reveal a strikingly sympathetic concern for their intellectual and emotional development, a kindly pedagogy that lasted well beyond the early childhood years.

Both for the sibling who is leader/teacher and for the follower/pupil sibling these experiences are likely to be important. We know that it is not only the experience of being taught that can have developmental consequence: the experiences of explaining and organizing and of confronting the puzzlement of a mind less mature than your own can be a formative one intellectually. Intellectual discussion between siblings—even if enjoyable for both—can have very different consequences for each. James Joyce "used" his brother Stanislaus's literary interests and wide reading, and their joint discussions, for his own special purposes. "He said frankly that he used me as a butcher uses his steel," Stanislaus commented, and indeed the knife-sharpening image of the fraternal relationship appears in *Ulysses*. "Where is your brother? Apothecaries Hall. My whetstone." The role of butcher and of whetstone could hardly be more different. For our present interest the significant general point is that the two children in such a relationship have different experiences within the family, and that these experiences can contribute to differences in the ways in which the children develop.

GROWING UP WITH A SIBLING WHO IS DIFFERENT FROM ONESELF

There is another, less direct way in which the presence of the sibling may lead to very different, developmentally important experiences for two children growing up together. It is not solely through the direct experience of interaction that the influence of a sibling can be felt by the other child. The continual presence of another child *different from oneself*, a child whom one knows all too well, and with whom one competes for parental affection and interest, can be profoundly important in the development of a sense of self, of emotional security, and of understanding others. As George Eliot put it in "Brother and Sister":

We had the self-same world enlarged for each
By loving difference of girl and boy.

Eliot is stressing the boy/girl differences, but the point is a more general one—that growing up with a sibling means growing up with a very different person.

There are two issues here. First, there is the individual's awareness of the other's personality, success, and relationships—the impact on self esteem of the comparison between self and sibling, private and internal though that comparison may be. Second, there is the impact of the other's *opinion* and *evaluation* of oneself—the explicit social comparison that we know plays a major role in the development of individual self-esteem and evaluation. The differences in personality between siblings mean that the impact of both processes—the private internal comparison of oneself with the other sibling and the knowledge of what the other thinks of one—will be different for two children in the family. We began this book with quotations from Mark Twain and from the James siblings that showed how vividly the writers were aware of the differences between them and their siblings. Mark Twain was highly conscious not only of the differences in his mother's relationship with himself and with Henry/Sid, but of the differences between the boys in personality and *goodness* that in part precipitated the maternal differentiation. Emily and Charlotte Brontë were evidently highly sensitive to the qualities of their brother Branwell that differed from their own, and as Leon Edel documents, Henry James was tortured by a preoccupation with comparing himself—unfavorably—with his brother William and strove continuously to achieve what William performed so effortlessly. William, to take one example of many, was a talented artist and drew with great accomplishment. Henry commented that "William drew because he could, while I did so in the main only because he did." He commented that he wished to live, if only "by the imagination, in William's adaptive skin."

Not only are such private self-comparisons with a sibling evident in much of the biographical and autobiographical material; the second process—the influence of the other's perception of oneself—is also often affectingly clear. Henry was all too aware of William's perception of his "limitations"; similarly the diary that Stanislaus Joyce kept as an adolescent shows how sensitive he was to his brother's view of him: "I perceive he regards me as quite commonplace and uninteresting—he makes no attempt at disguise—and though I follow him fully in this matter of opinion I cannot be expected to like it." James Joyce experienced no parallel insecurity in childhood and adolescence from his admiring brother's views of *him*.

In summary, the accounts of the relationships between the writers and their siblings indicate that differences in the experiences of the individual children within the relationship were frequently very marked. Both siblings were often strikingly sensitive to the differences between them and to their sibling's views. Are these differences within the relationship and this awareness of difference in personality and talent a reflection of the exceptional talents and sensitivities of the gifted individuals concerned? Can such differences in experiences within the sibling relationship be found in a wider population? Could these differences contribute to the differences in personality and development between siblings growing up within the same family?

We will begin with the experience of differences within the relationship, with evidence, as in the matter of parental differentiation discussed in the previous chapter, from a variety of sources: from interviews with siblings, from their parents' accounts of their behavior and relationships, and from observations of children in a range of settings.

DIFFERENCES IN CHILDREN'S VIEWS OF THEIR RELATIONSHIP WITH THEIR SIBLINGS

Considering first children's perceptions of their relationships with their siblings and whether they differ in their accounts of their experiences within the relationship, we will look both at the answers children give to specific questions about differences between them and their siblings in their behavior toward and feelings about one another, and at assessments of the quality of each sibling's feelings about the other derived from their free-flowing accounts of the relationship in response to more general questions. We now have the results of a number of studies of siblings ranging in age from middle childhood through young adulthood, which employed a questionnaire (the SIDE described in the previous chapter) in which the siblings were asked to compare their experience not only with their parents but within the sibling relationship itself. The SIDE sibling questions are included in table 5.1, along with scoring instructions and comparison data.

From these questionnaire studies of siblings from very diverse backgrounds, a consistent picture emerges. Many children see differences between themselves and their siblings in

Table 5.1 Sibling Inventory of Differential Experience (SIDE)
Interactions with Your Sibling

This questionnaire is designed to ask about your interactions with your sibling. Compare yourself to your sibling (or one of your siblings) when you were growing up and living at home. Scoring instructions and comparison scores are provided at the end of the questionnaire.

1 = My sibling has been much more this way than I have.
2 = My sibling has been a bit more this way than I have.
3 = My sibling and I have been the same in this way.
4 = I have been a bit more this way than my sibling.
5 = I have been much more this way than my sibling.

	Sibling Much More		Same		Me Much More
1) In general, who has started fights more often?	1	2	3	4	5
2) In general, who has shown more trust for the other?	1	2	3	4	5
3) In general, who has shown more concern and interest for the other?	1	2	3	4	5
4) In general, who has been more willing to help the other succeed?	1	2	3	4	5
5) In general, who has liked spending time with the other more?	1	2	3	4	5

Table 5.1 *(Continued)*

		Sibling Much More		Same		Me Much More
6)	In general, who has been more likely to take responsibility for the other?	1	2	3	4	5
7)	In general, who has been more stubborn with the other?	1	2	3	4	5
8)	In general, who has shown more confidence in the other?	1	2	3	4	5
9)	In general, who has acted more bitter toward the other?	1	2	3	4	5
10)	In general, who has compared him/herself with the other more?	1	2	3	4	5
11)	In general, who has been more likely to show feelings of anger to the other?	1	2	3	4	5
12)	In general, who has been more likely to feel superior over the other?	1	2	3	4	5
13)	In general, who has shown more understanding for the other?	1	2	3	4	5

Table 5.1 *(Continued)*

	Sibling Much More		Same		Me Much More
14) In general, who has been more likely to get jealous of the other?	1	2	3	4	5
15) In general, who has acted more kindly toward the other?	1	2	3	4	5
16) In general, who has been more likely to let the other down?	1	2	3	4	5
17) In general, who has shown more affection toward the other?	1	2	3	4	5
18) In general, who has been more likely to deceive the other?	1	2	3	4	5
19) In general, who has been more bossy toward the other?	1	2	3	4	5
20) In general, who has been more likely to want to get along well with the other?	1	2	3	4	5
21) In general, who has been more supportive of the other?	1	2	3	4	5

Table 5.1 *(Continued)*

	Sibling Much More		Same		Me Much More
22) In general, who has tried to outdo the other more?	1	2	3	4	5
23) In general, who has admired the other more?	1	2	3	4	5
24) In general, who has felt like the inferior one most?	1	2	3	4	5

Scoring: Four scales are scored: caretaking, jealousy, closeness, and antagonism:
   Caretaking: add items 3 + 4 + 6 + 12 + 19 + 21 and divide by 6.
   Jealousy: add items 5 + 10 + 14 + 22 + 23 + 24 and divide by 6.
   Closeness: add items 2 + 8 + 17 and divide by 3.
   For *antagonism,* items 13, 15, and 20 need to be "reversed," because a high score on these items implies *less* antagonism. To reverse items, if you entered a "3," leave it as a 3. If you reported "1," change it to "5." Similarly, if you reported "2," change it to "4"; change "4" to "2" and change "5" to "1." Once you have reversed the scores for items 13, 15, and 20, add items 1 + 7 + 9 + 11 + 13 + 15 + 16 + 18 + 20 and divide by 9.
   For the four scales, siblings in a large study yield the following average scores which you can use for purposes of comparing your scores: 2.6 for caretaking, 3.0 for jealousy, 3.1 for closeness, and 2.9 for antagonism. The extent to which your scores are below or above these averages indicates the degree to which you view your sibling relationship as *different* for the two of you.

all aspects of their interaction. The extent of the differences that the siblings describe is remarkable; it is much greater than the differences they report in parental treatment. Twenty percent of the children in one study described, on average, "much difference" in the dimensions of their own and their sibling's behavior within the relationship.

Do the siblings agree about the nature and extent of differences between them? In a sense the question is immaterial, given our concern with nonshared experiences; that they perceive differences is—as Henry James stressed—what is important. It is worth noting that siblings show some agreement about their interactions, although agreement is less for sibling interactions than it is about differential treatment by parents. Least agreement is seen for closeness—it is interesting that brothers and sisters not only do not feel the same about each other (recall Nancy and Carl with whom the chapter opened), but also do not always read each other's feelings well in this respect.

Are differences in siblings' interactions mediated by genetic differences between them? In the previous chapter, we saw that a twin and an adoption study using the SIDE disagreed as to the influence of genetics on parents' differential treatment of siblings. The studies agree that some slight genetic factors might lurk within differences in sibling interactions. For differential sibling interaction as reported on the SIDE, adoptive siblings show greater differences and identical twins show less difference than non-twin siblings or fraternal twins. More impressive than this evidence of genetic influence, however, is the magnitude of differences within pairs of identical twins, which cannot be due to genetic factors, because identical twins are identical genetically.

We obtain similar results from siblings' nondirected accounts of their relationship. In our Cambridge study we asked the children, aged on average 6 and 9 years, to talk more generally about their siblings and their feelings about them. ("Tell me about X. What is it you particularly like about X? What is it you particularly dislike about him/her?) The quotations from Nancy and Carl which opened this chapter came from this study. The children often gave us extensive and colorful answers, and—particularly relevant for our interest here—their comments on each other often differed notably. Sometimes the children differed in how friendly their comments were about each other, just as Carl and Nancy did. Here, for instance, are the comments of 6-year-old Sam and his older sister Molly:

> Sam: She's ugly. She's really, really ugly. She's not all that nice and I fight her.
> Molly: He lets me go in his gang . . . and he lets me go in his room and he lets me play with his toys . . . and he cleans my teeth, he gets the toothbrushes ready, and lets me help with his work and he lets me go in the shed. [Interviewer: What is it you like about him?] Playing with him. And I like him coming in my room except messing it up—he always does . . . and he plays with my toys.

Even when the two siblings were both very warm in their comments about the other, what they enjoyed about each other often differed. Elly, an older sister, said that she liked Carrie, her younger sister, "because she is really rather babyish and I like pretending she is my little baby and I like comforting her when she cries . . . and she says I'm beautiful now . . . " Carrie's comments were that "It's very nice with Elly . . . Elly is very nice—she taught me a lot of songs that she learned at Brownies 'cos she goes there. . . . She's just a very nice sister . . . the games she thinks of and plays with me and also there's another thing . . . the games we buy and that sort of thing."

We analyzed these responses according to the specific content of the comments and by the degree of "closeness" the children expressed, rated from both the kinds of comments made and the warmth of expression. (The rating of closeness proved highly reliable in terms of both rater agreement and test-retest assessment when the children were asked about their siblings again one month later.) The results showed marked differences between siblings in the closeness that they expressed toward the other: only 23 percent were rated as expressing similar degrees of closeness as their sibling.

The question of how significant these differences are to the children's outcome is obviously important, and we will take it up, after a look at several other sources of information about siblings.

PARENTS' VIEWS OF DIFFERENCES WITHIN SIBLING RELATIONSHIPS

He just worships her—he lights up when she comes in the room. But she can't really be bothered with him—he's really rather a nuisance to her.

Well, Amy does rather want to control and boss him—she's ever so pushy really towards him. He just fits in, mostly, with what she wants.
—(Two accounts from mothers of young siblings in the Cambridge studies)

The picture from our second source of information on the two participants in the sibling relationship—their parents—is similar to that painted by the children. In three studies—the Colorado Adoption Project, the Cambridge Sibling study, and a study of dual-earner families in Pennsylvania—parents were interviewed about their children's behavior and feelings toward each other, with very similar results. From the parents' answers to the detailed questions two general dimensions of the children's relationship with their sibling were derived, one a positive friendly dimension and the other a negative, hostile dimension. According to their parents' perceptions, 60 percent of the children in the Colorado study differed from their sibling in the extent and expression of their positive and friendly feelings and behavior toward that sibling. Siblings were perceived as somewhat more similar in their negative, hostile feelings and behavior, yet even so, 40 percent of children were reported to differ from their siblings in these hostile aspects of the relationship. That is, according to their parents, 60 percent of the children studied experienced different degrees of sibling friendliness and support than they showed toward their sibling, and 40 percent experienced differing degrees of hostility.

RESEARCHERS' OBSERVATIONS OF SIBLINGS

How does the information from *observations* of children interacting with their siblings fit with this picture from the reports of family members? We draw here on research that includes naturalistic studies of children (preschoolers, school children, and adolescents) in everyday family interaction and more structured studies of children videotaped while they play games or attempt to solve puzzles or tasks together. We might expect that in these latter situations differences between siblings in their behavior toward each other would be minimized, given the constraints of the settings in which the children are asked to play together. In spite of these constraints, differences in the two siblings' behavior are again clear, and again the differences are most marked in the positive, friendly aspects of their interaction, and in the dominance and control shown by the two individuals. Less difference in conflict behavior is perhaps unsurprising: if a row begins between two children in a constrained setting even the mildest and most patient child is likely to respond.

In the more free-flowing naturalistic observations, the differences between the siblings' behavior are clearer than in the more structured settings, often poignantly so, especially with the younger children. It is not uncommon for a 1 to 2-year-old younger sibling to approach repeatedly an irritated, uninterested older sibling with attempts to start joint play or with "helpful" overtures, only to be rebuffed time and time again, often with physical force. The mismatch of friendly initiations with hostile responses can be very high indeed in some families, in one recent study averaging 20 percent of interactions for the sample as a whole. Gluttons for punishment, the younger siblings appear to be. Such patterns of mismatch in emotional tone are not necessarily stable over the years. In one family in the Cambridge studies the younger sibling, a girl, took with equanimity repeated rejection of her friendly overtures and punishment from her brother during her second year. During two hours of observations when she was 24 months old, she made frequent friendly attempts to help or cooperate with him. He repulsed them all and continually teased or hurt her. Over the following months, her patient friendliness gradually decreased and was replaced by a fierce aggression. By the time she was 3 years old, the mismatch was reversed: her brother now was often the one to attempt cooperative play and she the negative partner. The worm had turned.

Sometimes the mismatch in affection and interest appears to grow when the older sibling's social life outside the family expands or becomes more intense. Interviews with parents confirm such a pattern. Compare the following two quotations from a mother in the Cambridge studies. In the first she describes how her two children got along when aged 5 and 3 years respectively; in the second she describes the same pair three years later.

> Oh they're ever so close. Carol [older sib] plays with her constantly and she [younger sib] loves it. They've got this game they play in the bedroom—it's to do with princesses, but I don't know what really happens—and they laugh and laugh. She [older sib] seems to really enjoy Annie. And Annie loves it.
> [Three years later:]
> Well you know Carol's off with her friends all the time now, and really doesn't want Annie tagging along. She gets quite fed up with her. . . . Annie'd still like to be part of the things they get up to . . . I think she's quite sad about it really—she loves it when Carol *will* play with her. But it's kind of one-sided . . . .

Children, then, perceive differences within their relationships with their siblings. Young siblings differ in their accounts of the closeness of the relationship; parents report differences; and observational studies reinforce the story that the family members tell. For one child in a family, growing up with a sibling can mean the irritating presence—day in, day out—of another child who demands attention, yet fails to play "properly," who manages to ruin any game, who whines and runs to Mommy whenever these inadequacies are pointed out, and who is always, most unfairly, championed by those partisan parents. For the other child in that same relationship, growing up with a sibling means an unrequited longing to play with the admired other, repeated failures to get the longed-for attention, a yearning admiration and desire to please that all too often fails. The story of Maggie Tulliver/Mary Anne Evans and her beloved brother Tom Tulliver/Isaac Evans is echoed in the patterns of mismatch in affection and interest from the systematic research on children and their siblings today. What the research shows us is that the case of Maggie and Tom is not an unusual story. The scale of differences in these sibling experiences, the studies suggest, may well be a potential source of differential influence for children within the same family.

LINKS TO OUTCOME

The important question for us is whether the difference in experience within the sibling relationship is linked to the children's outcomes. Preliminary investigations suggest that the answer to this question is, indeed, yes. Three studies have found associations between SIDE questions about differential sibling interactions and personality outcomes. For example, differential sibling jealousy predicts differences in emotionality—the sibling who has been the more jealous member of the pair is more emotional. Although it is plausible to think that such associations might be due to genetic differences between the siblings, similar associations have been found within pairs of identical twins, where the associations cannot be due to genetic factors.

The Colorado study has also related parental interviews and observations about sibling interactions to personality and adjustment outcomes. As discussed in the previous chapter, the extent of antisocial behavior and depression shown by 7-year-olds in the Colorado study was found to be linked to differential parent-child relationships. In a second set of analyses, we examined the contribution of differences in the siblings' experiences within their relationship to antisocial problem behavior and depressive moods among these children. The results showed that *differences* within the sibling relationship—assessed from both the mothers' accounts and from observations—were indeed related to the problem behaviors. For instance, the greater the disparity between the affection older siblings showed their younger siblings and the affection those younger siblings showed *them*, the more likely the older siblings were to be depressed in mood and antisocial in behavior. In the Cambridge study, the greater the disparity between the hostile behavior older siblings gave and what they received at the hands (often all too literally!) of their younger sibling, the lower their self-esteem.

SOCIAL COMPARISON

What about the other, less direct form of sibling influence we considered in the writers' lives with their siblings—the impact of growing up with a child who is very different from oneself? Sensitivity to the differences between oneself and one's sibling, and to that sibling's view of oneself is far from being a peculiarity of writers and their siblings. Studies of children within the wider community show that they are very conscious of differences between themselves and their siblings, and that they compare themselves with these different siblings surprisingly early in development. Although experimental studies of children in task situations where they are faced with solving problems find that children do not begin to compare their own performance and abilities with others until comparatively late in childhood (around age 7 or 8), a very different picture comes from studies of children within their families. Here processes of social comparison between siblings are apparent quite early. Not only is family discourse commonly replete with comparisons and evaluative judgments about the different family members, but children themselves make such judgments very early indeed, as the following example drawn from a study of siblings in Cambridge illustrates. Andy, a sensitive and rather anxious 30-month-old, overhears his mother's proud comment about his ebullient and exuberant younger sister Susie, who has just succeeded in achieving a (forbidden) goal in the face of prohibitions from her mother.

> Mother to Susie (affectionately): Susie you *are* a determined little devil!
> Andy to Mother (sadly): *I'm* not a determined little devil.
> Mother to Andy (laughing): No! What are you? A poor old boy!

Already at 2 ½ years Andy is becoming aware of how his sister is seen, of how she is likely to react and behave, and of how different he is from her.

Our observations of families with siblings include many incidents in which the children explicitly compare themselves with their siblings—sometimes they kindly explain to the observer just how different they are from their sibling! In the next example the older brother, 3 years old, commented with apparent glee on the likelihood of the baby's crying:

> Bruce S. (whose baby sib is playing with a balloon): He goin pop it in a minute. And he'll cry. And he'll be frightened of me too. I *like* the pop.

Older siblings, even those who were only 2 or 3 years old, often commented on their superior capabilities, as did Laura W. in our Cambridge study:

> Laura (to her baby brother Callum): You don't remember Judy. I do!
> [In a later observation:]
> Laura to her mother, who had commented to Callum on cutting teeth: I was cutting teeth. I was walking before he was. I walked before him.
> Laura to the observer: He's a walloper. He'll smack me when he's bigger. I'm going to be huge when he's a bit bigger. Up to the ceiling. Like you.
> Observer to Laura: I'm not up to the ceiling.
> Laura to observer: Well, I'll be up there. I'll grow so much. Up to the ceiling. So high.

Younger siblings, too, often compare themselves favorably with their older siblings, taking up with alacrity any opportunity in which older siblings referred to their own inadequacies, as the comments made by 47-month-old Sarah in the next example illustrate. Her brother, struggling with a homework report, was trying to get his mother to repeat (yet again) some facts that she had told him several times:

> Johnny to Mother: Oh oh I've forgotten what to write! Can you remind me?
> Mother to Johnny: No! Rethink it! Your memory's lacking.
> Johnny to Mother: I don't remember!
> Sarah to Johnny: *I* remember everything!
> Johnny to Sarah (sarcastically): OK tell me!
> Sarah to Johnny: Lalalala!
> Johnny to Sarah (unpleasantly): Oh you're smart!

What must be recognized is the huge importance of this consciousness of self and other—so vivid in the example of Andy and Susie—for children's development. Its significance lies in two different implications.

First, children's social lives and their relationships are transformed when they begin to understand what upsets, pleases, annoys another person, and how that other will react and behave. It is of enormous adaptive importance for children, born into a complex social world, to begin to grasp something of the feelings, motives, and intentions of the others who share that world. Given this adaptive importance, it is unsurprising that such understanding is high on the developmental agenda.

Second—and central to the question at the heart of this book—information about how others differ from oneself and what others think of oneself plays a crucial role in the way one's sense of self develops. It is here that the sibling differences take on major importance. Those differences mean that information about differences between oneself and the other, and its impact, will *differ* for the two children growing up together. George Eliot's nostalgic sonnet about her childhood stresses how her brother's understanding was enlarged through growing up with a younger, different, child by leading him to master his own impulses:

Widening its life with separate life discerned,
A Like unlike, a Self that self restrains.

In contrast, for her his presence meant the anchoring of her fantasies within a real world, and a focus on action and its consequences:

I knelt with him at marbles, marked his fling
Cut the ringed stem and make the apple drop,
Or watched him winding close the spiral string
That looped the orbits of the humming top.

Grasped by such fellowship my vagrant thought
Ceased with dream-fruit dream-wishes to fulfil;
My aery-picturing fantasy was taught
Subjection to the harder, truer skill

That seeks with deed to grave a thought-tracked line,
And by "What is," "What will be" to define.

The Cambridge studies in which we followed children through their second and third years showed just how early in childhood this awareness of the sibling's interests, feelings, and reactions develops, how salient for both children is the behavior of the other, and how adaptive it is for children to begin to understand what motivates and moves another child with whom they are growing up. The observations also brought to center stage the importance of emotion in these developments. Children learn, it seems, especially fast about what matters to them. Their most mature reasoning and questioning about the causes of others' behavior, for example, were apparent in situations of emotional saliency to them rather than in neutral settings. The behavior and emotional states of other family members are of particular importance and interest to them. For instance, in the Cambridge studies we examined the reaction of very young children to disputes between other family members. The youngest children that we studied were 14–16 months old, but already they were interested in any argument between their mothers and siblings. What particularly caught their attention and accounted for the differences in how they responded to disputes between others?—the emotion expressed by the antagonists.

A second line of evidence for these young children's curiosity about the feelings of their siblings and their mothers came from our analysis of children's questions about others. As they became more articulate during their third year, their questions about others were increasingly enquiries about the feelings of others. The social comparison that is apparent in this understanding of the other child is rarely affectively neutral. Rather, it can be fraught with emotion. Andy's comment on the difference between himself and his sister was hardly an emotionally neutral, detached remark.

From very different lines of enquiry, then, we find that children are aware of *differences* between themselves and their siblings in personality, confidence, and abilities, and of disparities in their experiences within the same relationship. These differences are of interest to them; indeed, they can be highly salient. What we have not yet traced are the intricacies of the developmental processes by which such awareness may contribute further to the differences between the siblings. It is clear that not only do children experience within the sibling relationship different degrees of affection, criticism, antagonism, and jealousy, but more indirectly the impact of the sibling's presence differs profoundly for each child. In the development of individual differences, both the experiences within the sibling relationship and the more indirect processes of social comparison are likely to be influential.

6

Beyond the Family

School parted us; we never found again
That childish world where our two spirits mingled.
 —George Eliot, "Brother and Sister"

When Charles Dickens's parents, in distressed circumstances, sent the 12-year-old Charles to work in a blacking factory, his life changed dramatically. He was thrust into a world in which he had to cope—very much on his own—with poverty, hunger, and all the stresses of working-class London life in the 1820s, and he drew on those experiences very directly in his novels; the impact of that depressing life on him as a young boy is vividly brought to us in *David Copperfield*. His world was "enlarged" in a way that differed greatly from the experience of his sister Fanny, who had become a student at the Royal College of Music. As we saw in chapter 4, that differentiation was a source of particular pain to him, but the change in his life had also a broader effect, by plunging him into a world of poor, working-class boys and men, a world in which he was humiliated and unhappy. His father was in the debtors' prison, and the effect on Charles of burdens that fell on him, but not on his sister Fanny, lasted a lifetime.

The Dickenses offer an extreme example of the differences in experience that are likely to affect all siblings as their world extends beyond the family. In commonsense terms, it seems extremely likely that when children begin to have a life beyond the family—at school, with friends, or beginning work (let's hope not in a blacking factory)—powerful new experiences, which *differ* for the siblings, will begin to influence their development.

In many nineteenth- and early twentieth-century middle-class families, when children were sent away to school their experiences of transition to a world beyond the family was traumatic. This change was not shared by all siblings, as some children were not sent away to school. It was of course not necessarily an unhappy change. Goethe, for example, writes affectionately in his autobiography of the childhood world and closeness he experienced with his younger sister Cornelia. This closeness came to an end when at age 16 he left Frankfurt for Leipzig to study. The experience was exhilarating for him—he celebrated it in letters and poems—but a major blow for her, a disaster that apparently set off a long-lasting depressive state. For George Eliot, as we saw in the last chapter, the beginning of her brother's school days marked a crucial transition in their shared experiences. For Rudyard Kipling, the power of school experiences is captured in his *Stalky and Co.* and in *Something of Myself;* his sister had no such school life. Such instances are numerous in the lives of those who grew up in the previous century.

These examples raise a series of questions about the impact of influential experiences beyond the family for children today. First, there are some relatively straightforward descriptive issues. How different are children's experiences with friends and peers from those of their siblings? Or their encounters and relationships with other important adults? How different are their experiences of transitions from home to school or between school and the adult world of work? Beyond such descriptive queries we move to questions more difficult to answer: How far do these differences in experiences beyond the family contribute to personality differences, to differences in delinquency and in emotional adjustment? How far are they, rather, the consequences of already established personality characteristics? And finally we face some of the most intractable developmental issues that psychologists have to tackle: Do experiences outside the family in middle childhood, adolescence, and adulthood have less impact than the *early* childhood experiences on which much of the past theorizing on development has concentrated? Are differences in within-the-family experiences more important in development than differences in siblings' lives with friends and peers or adults outside the family? The possibility that nonshared experiences in adulthood—well beyond the childhood period that has been the primary focus of most developmental research—play a crucial role in the formation of individual differences has to be considered.

In this chapter we discuss these questions, necessarily from a base of information that is very small—especially for the final set of questions. It is important to recognize that most experiences outside the family are likely to be specific to each sibling. What this means is that in a vast, and relatively unexplored territory, any of the significant landmarks may be "nonshared." Indeed the key point from which we started this exploration is that if such environmental factors do influence development, they must be specific to each child, and they must be nonshared.

How can we begin to map such a huge uncharted landscape? For it is, surprisingly, a terrain that, as far as individual differences in development are concerned, is largely unexplored. We know something about the impact of normative changes, such as marriage or parenthood, and about the differences between groups of people in experiences outside the family, such as broad social-class differences. In the matter of explaining individual differences in the influence of such events we are still very much wandering in the dark. We are especially ignorant about differences between siblings in the influence of experiences beyond the family, though for peers, at least, we have some descriptive information as a starting point. For our first steps exploring these issues, it makes sense to begin with the first relationships that children form outside their families, those with peer groups.

PEERS

Do siblings growing up together in Western cultures today have similar experiences in their relationships with other children outside the family? Psychologists increasingly emphasize the role of peers in development, not only in the area of delinquency and deviance (where there is good evidence that peers are an important influence independent of parent, school, or neighborhood, an influence that increases with age between middle childhood and adulthood) but in social development more broadly considered. Expanding Piaget's argument that peers play a special role in social and moral understanding, many psychologists now suggest that peers can have considerable influence on the development of self-esteem, emotional adjustment, and social competence. If we take these arguments seriously, and there is increasing evidence showing that we should, then the question of whether siblings have similar or different experiences with peers takes on particular prominence in the exploration of nonshared experiences beyond the family.

At first sight it might be thought that siblings' experiences with peers might be rather similar. After all, they do share neighborhood and social background, and frequently attend the same school. Their parents' attitude to their extrafamilial social life is not, we might suppose, going to differ drastically from child to child within the family. But siblings tell us quite a different story. The SIDE—the questionnaire that we have described in previous chapters—includes twenty-six questions focusing on children's experiences with peers, and the results of a study using this measure with siblings show that 20 percent of children report that their sibling's peer group and peer relationships are much different from their own. A further 42 percent of children report "a bit of difference" in their peer group characteristics. Two different studies have now found that these differences that siblings report in their peer experiences are as great as those they report in their experiences with their siblings—and considerably greater than the differences in parental treatment that they describe. The extent of difference varies somewhat with the particular aspect of the children's peer group experiences that are under scrutiny. For aspects of delinquency and use of drugs and alcohol, siblings' peer groups are more similar than they are in their attitude to college or school work or in the kind of popularity that is valued.

As in the previous chapters on parents and siblings, we include the SIDE items relevant to our discussion (see table 6.1). At the end of the items are scoring instructions and average scores for a large sample of siblings for purposes of comparison. You might also wish to review your SIDE scores

Table 6.1   Sibling Inventory of Differential Experience (SIDE)
Interactions with Peer Groups

Think of each item as if your peer group (your main group of friends) has a personality of its own. Even though friends inside each peer group might be quite different, think about how the group is in general. Think about your experience and that of one of your siblings when you were growing up and living at home. Scoring instructions and comparison scores are provided at the end of the questionnaire.

1 = My sibling has had a peer group much more like this than my peer group.

2 = My sibling has had a peer group a bit more like this than my peer group.

3 = My sibling and I have had the same type of peer group in this way.

4 = I have had a peer group which is a bit more like this than my sibling's peer group.

5 = I have had a peer group which is much more like this than my sibling's peer group.

	Sibling's Peers Much More		Same		My Peers Much More
1) popular	1	2	3	4	5
2) ambitious	1	2	3	4	5
3) outgoing	1	2	3	4	5
4) lazy	1	2	3	4	5
5) hard working	1	2	3	4	5
6) intelligent	1	2	3	4	5
7) mature	1	2	3	4	5
8) extraverted	1	2	3	4	5
9) delinquent	1	2	3	4	5
10) responsible	1	2	3	4	5
11) successful	1	2	3	4	5
12) friendly	1	2	3	4	5
13) rebellious	1	2	3	4	5

Table 6.1 *(Continued)*

	Sibling's Peers Much More		Same		My Peers Much More
14) conforming	1	2	3	4	5
15) well adjusted	1	2	3	4	5

Circle the appropriate number for each interest below. Friends inside peer groups may have had separate interests, but rate the activity that best describes what the group has liked to do in general.

1 = My sibling has had a peer group much more interested in this than my peer group.

2 = My sibling has had a peer group a bit more interested in this than my peer group.

3 = My sibling and I have had the same type of peer group with this same interest.

4 = I have had a peer group a bit more interested in this than my sibling's peer group.

5 = I have had a peer group much more interested in this than my sibling's peer group.

	Sibling's Peers Much More		Same		My Peers Much More
16) going on to college	1	2	3	4	5
17) achieving in school	1	2	3	4	5
18) student government	1	2	3	4	5
19) "partying," drinking, etc.	1	2	3	4	5
20) illicit drugs (such as marijuana)	1	2	3	4	5

Table 6.1 *(Continued)*

	Sibling's Peers Much More		Same		My Peers Much More
21) political and social issues	1	2	3	4	5
22) achieving "status" in social situations	1	2	3	4	5
23) having a boyfriend or girlfriend	1	2	3	4	5
24) likely to skip class	1	2	3	4	5
25) likely to get along well	1	2	3	4	5
26) likely to be called the "bad" crowd	1	2	3	4	5

Scoring: Three peer group characteristic scales are scored: college orientation, popularity, and delinquency.

College Orientation: add items 2 + 5 + 6 + 7 + 10 + 11 + 15 + 16 + 17 + 18 + 21 + 25 and divide by 12.

Popularity: add items 1 + 3 + 8 + 12 + 22 + 23 and divide by 6.

For *delinquency*, item 14 needs to be "reversed," because a high score on this item implies *less* delinquency. To reverse the item, if you entered a "3," leave it as a 3. If you reported "1," change it to "5." Similarly, if you reported "2," change it to "4"; change "4" to "2" and change "5" to "1." Once you have reversed your score for item 14, add items 4 + 9 + 13 + 14 + 19 + 20 + 24 + 26 and divide by 8.

For the three scales, siblings in a large study yield the following average scores which you can use for purposes of comparing your scores: 3.3 for college orientation, 3.1 for popularity, and 3.0 for delinquency.

from the previous chapters and compare those for parents, siblings, and peers.

Twin and adoption studies using the SIDE suggest some genetic influence on the selection of and by peers. In the twin study mentioned in previous chapters, fraternal twins reported peer differences just as great as non-twin siblings even though fraternal twins are the same age. Peer groups of identical twins, however, are less different than peer groups of fraternal twins. Although this finding suggests that genetic factors affect selection of peer groups, it is possible that identical twins, who are not only the same age but are also difficult to distinguish physically, select and are selected by peer groups in ways that do not generalize to other siblings. In a comparison between SIDE peer scores for biological and adoptive siblings, the adoptive siblings reported somewhat greater peer differences than biological siblings, further implicating genetic influence. The fact that even identical twins report peer differences on the SIDE provides strong evidence that nonshared environmental factors are involved in the differences in siblings' peer groups.

In these studies, the initial steps have also been taken towards answering our second set of questions, those concerned with the connections between these differential peer experiences and individual differences in personality and adjustment. We find associations between the siblings' personality differences and differences in their experiences with peers. What is particularly interesting is that these differential experiences are associated not just with differences between the siblings (the more sociable sibling, for instance, enjoying more peer popularity, and the more anger-prone sibling associating with peers who have a different attitude to college) but with the personality of the individual compared to other individuals in the wider population. The message is this: if we want to explain why individuals in the general population differ from one another in personality, we have to take account of their individual peer experiences as children—experiences not shared with siblings.

Are these differences in experience with peers the consequence of personality and adjustment differences, or do they contribute to causing such differences? We do not yet know. The studies so far carried out are cross-sectional and cannot bring longitudinal analyses to bear on this important question. Could a third factor, genetics, be responsible for the association? As we have seen, genetics may influence the SIDE measure of peers. Since the association between sibling differences in peer relationships and differences in personality (especially extraversion) and adjustment (especially sense of well-being) emerges for identical twins, the differences, and their links across relationships, cannot be entirely explained by genetics.

Our guess is that both causal processes are likely to be important. Children with easy-going, sociable personalities will probably be more popular when they first move into a world of peers than their shyer, more anxious siblings, but we know too that good experiences with peers have a "positive feed-back" effect on children's confidence with other children and on their sense of self-esteem.

The SIDE interview focuses on the nature of children's experiences with a group of others of the same age rather than on children's intimate friendships. But it seems a priori very likely that differences in friendship experiences may be just as important, if not more important, than differences in the peer group with whom siblings associate. Here is an incredibly important aspect of children's lives outside the family for which nothing is known about sibling differences.

In summary, this first set of systematic information about siblings' experiences beyond the family shows us that even within childhood, children's social experiences outside the family differ from those of their siblings, that some of these differences in experience are systematically related to their personality and adjustment, and that they are also linked to nonshared experiences within the family. To explain individual differences in the quality of friendships of children within the population, we have to take account of the differences in their experiences within the family from those of their siblings.

Peer relationships are only one set of a multitude of potential influences on children's development that exert their effects outside the family. Common sense, as well as systematic studies, underline the power of teachers and other "significant" adults in the lives of children and adolescents, of sexual relationships and dating, of work experiences, and of the experience of becoming a spouse and a parent. Our examination of siblings' relationships with their teachers, for example, shows that siblings have strikingly different relationships with their teachers. Life-span psychologists have shown how important it is to take proper account of the nature and timing of these influences in an individual's life; they have shown, too, how their significance can vary for different historical "cohorts." The timing and significance of marriage and work, for example, are clearly very different for girls in the 1980s than they were for girls in the Depression. But to what extent are these myriad possible influences *different* in their impact on siblings? What is the relative significance of the different nonshared experiences for the development of individual differences in adjustment, delinquency, or the quality of adult relationships? How far do different cohorts of siblings differ in the degree to which their experiences beyond the family are nonshared? These are questions on which we have desperately little information. Rather than speculating on possible answers in the absence of

125

research on sibling differences we will focus on two themes in current developmental research that might guide our attempts to explore this newfound land. One overarching theme stands out.

ENVIRONMENTAL INFLUENCES IN LATER CHILDHOOD DEVELOPMENT

It is now acknowledged, and well documented, that experiences in middle childhood, adolescence, and adulthood can be profoundly important in development. The malleability and adaptability of developmental processes is increasingly clearly understood, and ideas on development have shifted from simple notions that what happens early in development inevitably has more impact than later experience. The thrust of some of the most exciting developmental research in progress now is to document the extent to which particular experiences later in development can modify or ameliorate the impact of early experience.

Consider as a dramatic example a study by Michael Rutter and his colleagues at the Institute of Psychiatry in London. A group of women who had spent their early years in institutions, without the security of a warm attachment relationship to a parent figure, were traced as adults. Those women who had 2-year-old children were studied, with the focus on whether early experiences within the institution were linked to difficulties the women themselves had as parents, and whether experiences in the intervening years affected their relationship with their children or their parenting style. The study has generated a host of interesting findings and taught us many lessons about development; the point to be stressed here is that although the women who had experienced institutional life as children did indeed have more problems in parenting than a control group, both the women's adolescent experiences and the quality of their spousal relationship were also important in predicting some of the features of their parenting behavior. Women whose spouses were supportive and well adjusted, for instance, had many fewer problems as parents *in spite of their early childhood experiences* than the women whose spouses were less supportive and less well adjusted.

The question that is difficult to answer from this study is how far differences in the women's personalities shaped these later experiences. Were the women who formed relationships with well-adjusted spouses themselves in better shape or more secure in personality than the women whose men turned out to be disasters as spouses and fathers? Were the good experiences in adolescence that were associated with better outcomes in adulthood the consequence of differences in the women's personalities rather than an independent source of influence? This puzzle highlights the value of studying siblings through developmental stages, to clarify the contributions to differences in their experiences and relationships beyond childhood. Like several of the other major studies that follow individuals from childhood to adulthood, the study of women who spent their childhood in institutions not only raised some puzzling questions, but gives some useful guidelines. From such research, as well as from common sense, we can document the effects of these beyond-childhood experiences in the formation of differences in adulthood—pinpointing certain adolescent experiences and the spousal relationship as especially significant. These bring us to a second developmental theme that has emerged from studies of the life course.

TRANSITION POINTS IN THE LIFE COURSE

In the study of the previously institutionalized women, differences between them as adolescents in how they dealt with the transition from the world of school to that of work turned out to be particularly illuminating. The girls who as adolescents had some plans for their future life were more likely, several years later, to be coping well as parents and to have supportive spouses. Their example supports an idea that has been suggested by a number of developmental studies: that transition points in peoples' lives, such as the start of schooling, the move from school to the adult work world, or the transition to parenthood are of special significance.

We should not assume that such transitions are necessarily or universally stressful or significant in their impact. Rather, differences in how people go through such changes in their lives, and in the timing of these transitions, may reveal points on an individual trajectory that set new directions in a person's life. Studies by Avshalom Caspi, Glen Elder, and Daryl Bem have shown particularly vividly that the timing with which an individual joins the adult work world or marries has a continuing impact on his or her later life—but that the personality of the individual affects this matter of timing. Boys who were shy and reserved in late childhood, for instance, were more likely than their peers to make a late entry into marriage, parenthood, and stable careers. The researchers stress the progressive accumulation of the consequences of these experiences—"cumulative continuity" is the phrase they use to describe the patterns they trace. The significance of this emphasis on transitions by the life-span psychologists for our concern with the development of individual differences is this: differences between siblings in how such transitions are accomplished, in their timing and in their impact, may be particularly important in setting siblings off on different trajectories.

For instance, in the James family, the move to Europe that Henry (the father) organized when William and Henry (the son) were 14 and 12 years old, respectively, had enormously important consequences for Henry especially. It marked the beginning of his "cultivated cosmopolitanism" and a lifetime of exploring the intricacies of cultural differences between Europeans and Americans and the power of such differences to influence peoples' lives. In contrast, for Alice, their sister who was only 7, the change had much less impact, according to the biographer Edel, since at that age the cultural experience inevitably had less force for her.

Our studies of children today include several similar examples. One family in Cambridge, for instance, moved to another part of England when the older sister was 7 and the younger brother was 3. The move was an easy experience for the boy, whose world was still a family one, but the girl had major troubles settling into a new school where she found herself an outcast from a tight in-group of girls. Her troubled reaction led to her being labeled by these girls in an unfavorable way, and this reputation followed her for several rather unhappy years.

The pattern of *cumulative* experience that certain changes or transitions set off brings us to an issue that, again, the life-span psychologists have emphasized: the notion that as we live our lives, experiences accumulate and thus increasingly account for differences between us. The implication of this hypothesis, put forward by Paul Baltes of the Max Planck Institute on Human Development in Berlin, is that environmental influences become increasingly important throughout the life span and that genetic effects become correspondingly less important. We now see a further implication—namely that *nonshared* experience becomes increasingly important in later life. Of relevance here is the general finding in gerontological research that variance between individuals increases later in life. That is, contrary to images suggested by the pigeonholing of older individuals with terms such as *"the* elderly," older people actually show greater individuality than younger individuals. Perhaps individuals experience environments that are *not shared* to an increasing extent as they age, and this increase in nonshared environment is responsible for the increase in variance. To what extent does behavioral genetic research show changes in nature and nurture later in life?

NONSHARED ENVIRONMENT
THROUGH THE LIFE COURSE

No definitive answers can be given to such questions because so little research in behavioral genetics has considered the second half of the life course, from middle adulthood to old age. In fact, other than a twin study in the 1940s in New York that focused on issues of health and longevity, there is only one behavioral genetic study of the later adult years. The Swedish Adoption/Twin Study of Aging (SATSA) uses the most powerful design in the armamentarium of behavioral genetics for a sample whose average age is 60. SATSA is a twin study that compares identical and fraternal twins, and it is also an adoption study in that twins reared apart are compared to twins reared together. As described in chapter 2, when identical twin correlations exceed fraternal twin correlations, genetic influence is implicated. Comparisons between correlations for twins reared together and apart directly measure the sum influence of being reared together, the environmental influence that we call shared environment. A register of nearly 25,000 twin pairs in Sweden included hundreds of pairs of twins reared apart whose average age is now over 60 years; twins reared together were matched to these twins reared apart. Although twins are seldom separated at birth any longer, fifty to seventy years ago worldwide epidemics, economic depression, and high rates of death of the mother during childbirth were responsible for the relatively frequent separation of twins early in life. In some years, as many as 1 percent of all twins born in Sweden were separated. Half of the sample of separated twins in SATSA were separated during the first two years of life, 85 percent were separated by 5 years of age, and the rest were separated before they were 10 years old.

Although science depends on replication, the design and sample size of this single study give us some confidence in its results. For personality, which has been the focus of the study to date, SATSA results provide some support for the life-span specialists' hypothesis of increasing influence of nonshared environment and decreasing heritability. Nonshared environment accounts for about 60 percent of the variance as compared to about 55 percent in studies of younger adults, and heritability is about 30 percent on average rather than 40 percent. Are these differences so small as to be trivial? No: few findings in the behavioral sciences account for as much as 10 percent of variance, and these differences involve 5 percent and 10 percent of the variance. We can say with confidence that nonshared environment is at least as important later in life as it is earlier in the life course; and it appears to become more important during the adult years.

If nonshared environment accounts for about 60 percent of the variance and heritability accounts for 30 percent, what is responsible for the rest of the variance? Herein might lie an interesting story. This Swedish study provides a strong test of the importance of shared rearing environment, because the twins who were reared together can be compared with those reared apart. It also tests the importance of the shared environments of adult life by examining with model-fitting analyses the extent of twin similarity that is not explained by shared rearing environment in childhood or by heredity. The investigators in the SATSA study expected to find that shared family environment, already of weak influence early in life, would have very little effect on personality decades later during the last half of the life span. They also expected to find that a different type of shared environment, namely those experiences that were shared by siblings during adult life after they had left their childhood home, would increase in importance.

The SATSA researchers were surprised by their results on both counts. First, shared adult experiences showed little effect, meaning that the effects of adult twins on each other or shared experiences in adulthood do not contribute to twin similarity later in life, independently of the effects of shared heredity and shared rearing environments. Second, and even more surprising, is the finding that shared rearing environment accounted for about 10 percent of the variance of personality later in life. This suggests the interesting possibility that shared rearing environment has an effect on personality decades later even though it has little effect while siblings are growing up together in the same family.

Despite this possible sleeper effect of shared childhood experiences, the effects of nonshared environmental influences remain dominant. Recent findings from the SATSA project suggest two novel ways in which nonshared experiences are important later in life. The Swedish twins were studied a second time after a three-year interval in order to begin to assess the role of genetic and environmental factors on change as well as on continuity during later life. Personalities appear to have remained quite stable during the three-year period, consistent with longitudinal studies in earlier adulthood that found substantial stability over three and four decades. What causes this stability? It appears that the combinations of genetic and environmental influences that are responsible for variation at a particular age are responsible in equal proportions for continuity from age to age. That is, nonshared environment accounts for more than half of the similarity in twins as they move from age to age; genetic factors account for the rest of the covariation. In other words, not only does nonshared environment contribute importantly to who we are at a given age, it is also the major reason why we stay the way we are. Genetic factors are importantly involved in age-to-age continuity, but shared environment plays no role at all.

The second finding relevant to our concern with nonshared experiences involves change rather than continuity—there is some personality change during the life course despite its considerable continuity. Among the Swedish twins, the personality changes that were found to have occurred during the three-year period were entirely the result of differences in environmental experience. That is, genetic influence contributes only to continuity but nonshared environment contributes to change as well as to continuity. Perhaps this is not suprising, when we consider the major life events that might change personality later in life. One's retirement, illness, and death of one's spouse and friends are not likely to have nearly as great an impact on one's sibling as on oneself.

Stepping back from these specifics, we can see a larger significance of the SATSA results in the impetus they provide to thinking about nonshared environment beyond the family in a life-span perspective from womb to tomb.

7

Chance

I look upon the factors that helped me to fulfil [my fate] as so many fortunate strokes of chance. The family pattern followed by my parents required that they should have another child quite soon; and as chance would have it, this child was a girl. Would things have turned out differently for me if it had been a boy? . . . I do not think I should have benefitted. . . . Chance, in one form or another, helped me to fill my life with people. . . . Chance favoured me extraordinarily in placing Sartre upon my path.

—Simone de Beauvoir, *All Said and Done*

Simone de Beauvoir emphasized repeatedly the role chance played in shaping her life and experiences so differently from her sister's. The significance of chance in making brothers and sisters different was clearly seen by Francis Galton, who anticipated by a century the finding that nonshared environment is the primary source of environmental influences in development:

Circumstance comprises all the additional accidents, and all the peculiarities of nurture both before and after birth, and every influence that may conduce to make the characteristics of one brother differ from those of another.

Galton also thought that nonshared environment was primarily chance, which he called circumstance, and noted that chance can produce long-lasting effects:

> The whimsical effects of chance in producing stable results are common enough. Tangled strings variously twitched, soon get themselves into tight knots.

Galton's prescience in matters of nature and nurture suggests that we should also pay special attention to his views on the role of chance in the creation of sibling differences. Because so little is known empirically about the effect of chance on development, this chapter will necessarily be brief.

Indeed, although everyone has some intuitions about chance, it is difficult to define. The Oxford English Dictionary has trouble defining *chance* as well as the many other words that signal our concern about such things. The origins of the word *luck* are obscure, but it was probably introduced from the German as a gambling term. *Fortune* and *fortuitious* have been around for centuries—in 1374, Chaucer wrote that "fortune is my foe." The list is long, including *accident, adventitious, contingency, fate, haphazard,* and *random.* One of the most interesting words is *caprice,* shortened from *capriccio;* one of its earliest recorded uses was in 1600, in Shakespeare's *As you Like It,* where it connoted "goatlike," in the sense of goats scampering along the hill tops. Good luck is so important in science that a word is used to refer specifically to the role of chance in scientific discovery: *serendipity,* derived by Horace Walpole at the turn of the century from a Persian fable called *The Three Princes of Serendip,* which referred to Ceylon, now Sri Lanka. The word was revived in 1940 in a famous paper on discovery and chance by Walter Cannon.

CHANCE

We use the word *chance* to denote low probability, unpredictable events over which an individual has little control. These are relative criteria. Automobile accidents are called accidents because they are assumed to be due to chance, even though their probability is not very low and they are both somewhat predictable and controllable. As the probability, predictability, and controllability of an event increases, we agree that an event is not chance: it is not just bad luck when a drunk driver crashes.

Chance in this sense was *tuche* to the Greek philosophers and contrasted with *techne,* a word that referred to the ability to control one's destiny. For the early Greek tragic poet/philosophers Aeschylus and Sophocles, *tuche* was a critical element of life. Their tragedies show good people being ruined by things that just happen to them. These themes seem foreign, now, because we like our plots to be rational—a taste that grew from the tremendous impact of Plato and, later, Kant on Western culture. Plato's conception of the life of reason was essentially an attempt to make humans immune to caprice. In his *Republic,* the most perfect human life was one devoted to furthering control over contingency by learning and the contemplation of truth. *Tuche* had no place in this Platonic world. Aristotle tried to redress the imbalance between *tuche* and *techne,* but Kant and subsequent philosophers all but erased *tuche* from our cultural heritage.

Although Freud's name is associated with the exploration of the irrational, he did not address the issue of chance in his work, but searched for rational explanations of seemingly irrational behavior. Similarly, the chaos theory currently fashionable in many areas of science is an attempt to find order in disorder. Although the word *chaos* implies randomness, the point of chaos theory is that, in nonlinear dynamic systems

137

such as weather, apparent randomness can be described by simple equations.

Sometimes, however, things just happen—*tuche*. Biographies are full of examples of chance events that are turning points in lives. Chance can be writ large, as in the case of major illnesses or accidents or war experiences that dramatically alter the course of an individual's development. The death of a parent appears frequently in our nineteenth-century writers' lives as a crucial turning point.

More surprising are the often seemingly trivial chance events that launch lives in slightly different directions with cascading effects as time goes by. One of our favorite examples comes from the autobiography of Charles Darwin:

> The voyage of the *Beagle* has been by far the most important event in my life, and has determined my whole career; yet it depended on so small a circumstance as my uncle offering to drive me thirty miles to Shrewsbury, which few uncles would have done, and on such a trifle as the shape of my nose.

Darwin's comment about his nose refers to the quixotic captain of the *Beagle*, Captain Fitz-Roy, who nearly rejected Darwin for the trip because the shape of his nose indicated to Fitz-Roy that Darwin would not possess sufficient energy and determination for the voyage. Darwin wrote that, during the voyage, Fitz-Roy became convinced that "my nose had spoken falsely."

The recent autobiography of the French geneticist François Jacob, who won a Nobel prize for his research on the regulation of DNA, adds to the long list of possible examples. Partially crippled from wounds received during the Normandy invasion, after the war Jacob drifted through jobs in journalism and film making. He met a young man who piqued his interest in genetic research. Chance struck again: although untrained, Jacob was accepted into the laboratory of a famous biologist, because, according to Jacob, the biologist had earlier that day made an important discovery that put him in a good mood. Jacob notes, "Had I been he, I would surely not have accepted into my laboratory a chap like myself."

CHANCE AND SIBLING DIFFERENCES

Chance events are particularly interesting in the present context because they are a likely source of differences between siblings. Illness or accidents suffered by one child in a family, as in the case of Henry James's mysterious "obscure hurt," or particular experiences outside the family, such as school problems or friendships, are examples of events that affect one sibling but not the other.

One might think that just by definition chance could not be shared by siblings. Rudyard Kipling's unusual school experiences had a profound impact on him and on his writing, "teaching him to live in the world of action and still be himself," as noted by his biographer. These experiences had no part in his sister's life, any more than Charles Dickens's experiences of factory life were part of his sister Fanny's. However, some important chance events are shared by siblings. A shared event can occur within a family, as when a parent dies early or suffers mental illness, or it can occur within a culture, as in the case of economic depression or war. Yet such apparently shared chance events may be experienced very differently by siblings, because the siblings will differ in developmental stage and in personality. In 1888, Virginia Woolf and all her siblings were attacked by whooping cough. Virginia, at 6, was very ill and took much longer than her three siblings to recover. Her convalescence was marked, according to her biographer Bell, by an intellectual revolution: "At the age of six she had become a rather different kind of person, more thoughtful and more speculative."

In one of our studies of siblings in Cambridge, the impact of many events that appear at first glance to have been shared by the siblings—such as a mother's serious illness, or a father's unemployment—was found to be often very different for the two children. We studied the effect of a range of potentially stressful events or situations, including changes in housing, in parental employment and finances, in propinquity to relatives, and in the health of different family members; accidents; and problems at school. The impact of each of these events on each sibling was assessed by a child psychiatrist. The results showed that 69 percent of the events that had negative impacts on children in the study had *different* effects on the two siblings. For instance, one mother suffered from stress-related attacks of anxiety for which she was treated by a psychologist. Her firstborn son was much affected and became a very worried child; her secondborn daughter was much less concerned. In another family, the father was forced, because he had lost his job, to move away from home for several months. This had a greater impact on his secondborn son than on his older daughter. Another mother was diagnosed as suffering from leukemia. Her second child was much more affected by this than was her first child.

The most frequently occurring life events that had severe negative impacts on the children were events that beset one child rather than both, such as accidents or illness, or stressful school problems, often associated with school change as in the example quoted in the last chapter. Important for our concern with understanding differences in individual outcomes is, first, that two children growing up in the same family had such different experiences of stressful events, and second, that these events were systematically related to later differences in outcome. It is a notorious problem with research on the influence of life events that the impact of an event is not independent of the personality—the vulnerability—of the person affected. Thus such events can rarely be regarded as "external" factors, affecting emotional adjustment or self-esteem in any independent or straightforwardly causal manner.

The important point here is that within the same family two children will usually experience differing degrees of stress. Stressful events can have a cumulative, cascading effect, and the experience of a series of such events may well make an individual increasingly vulnerable and likely to suffer greater negative impact from future events. Starting from initial differences in personality, then, very different trajectories of suffering from stressful "chance" events can occur.

Consider the events that occurred in one family in the Cambridge study. The father had to be away for a three-month stretch for his job. His firstborn son missed him considerably, much more so than a younger girl. Over the following eighteen months the family was involved in two car accidents, a burglary, and a house move. In one of the accidents, the driver of the other car was killed; both children were in the car, but it was the firstborn who was markedly affected by the experience. He became particularly anxious about his parents when they went out. The family house was burgled a second time, and again it was the firstborn child who was disturbed by the event. Finally, the paternal grandfather, to whom the firstborn was very attached, died—and again the boy was very much affected. His sister, in contrast to the increasing disturbance shown by her brother, weathered these events with little signs of upset other than a brief, immediate response.

An account of another child, given by a mother of two children in Cambridge, tells a similar story of cumulative troubles for a young girl that did not affect her sister in the same way at all:

> Well, she's had a series of things that were hard to take this year—she takes things so much harder than Katy anyway—and it just seems like a pile-up of troubles for her. First, she didn't get on with her new teacher this year (well actually neither of them got the teacher they wanted, but Katy didn't mind so much), then her best friend Sarah left Cambridge. Now we have weekends when she just mopes around *and* she doesn't do the school work, so that means more trouble at school. She's not been picked for a couple of things at school . . . that's probably the result of all the other troubles. . . . She seems a real misery these days.

What about events that happen separately to each sibling, such as an injury caused by falling off a swing? Obviously, there are no *schlimazel* (Yiddish for "crooked luck") genes that attract life's pies in the face. But genetic differences can affect personality and these differences can, for example, predispose some children to be reckless sensation-seekers who put themselves at greater risk for accidents by playing with fire. That is, "accidents will happen" but they will happen more often to some children than others and to some sibling pairs more than others. In other words, accidents are not completely chance events. Once you begin to think about chance in this way, it becomes plausible that siblings experience in tandem many events that might otherwise be thought of as chance—such as embarrassing incidents at school or falling in with bad companions. Personality similarities of siblings can lead to similar experiences. Physical similarity may be important as well. Although the noses of Darwin's siblings were unlikely to lead them to experiences similar to his encounter with the capricious Captain Fitz-Roy, it is possible that variables such as physical appearance lead siblings to have similar, apparently chance, encounters. Studies of chance events in siblings' lives will be required to sort out these possibilities.

Research on the occurrence and impact of life events in adults is also relevant. The literature on major and minor life events sprawls over thousands of articles since its modern origins in the 1960s. The source of this intense research interest lies in the association between life events and stress, and the use of this association for predicting mental illness. The research began by compiling long lists of things that happen to people, including positive events (marriage, promotion, birth of a child) as well as negative events (death of a relative, divorce) and events that could be positive or negative for different people (moving house). Events weighted for their stressfulness are summed to yield total life events scores, and these scores are used to predict psychopathology. The results suggest unsurprisingly that, although positive events like marriage may be quite stressful, prediction of psychopathology depends to a greater extent on negative events. Again, we need to know how similarly or differently siblings experience these negative events before we can assess how far they are specific to one individual, and thus contribute to the differences between people in outcome.

Another distinction has recently emerged that is especially relevant to our theme. Uncontrollable life events are thought to drive people crazy to a greater extent than controllable events. Uncontrollable events include illness or death of a family member; in contrast, conflict with family members is an example of a controllable event. The distinction between controllable and uncontrollable life events arose from work on a topic that was termed "learned helplessness." When individuals feel that they have no control over what happens to them, they begin to behave in an increasingly "helpless" way—they learn to be helpless. This helplessness can lead to depression and to a breakdown in immune system functioning and thereby can cause physical illness. An uncontrollable event is largely what we mean by chance. Recent work on learned helplessness suggests that people differ in their susceptibility to uncontrollable events, to a large extent because of differences in optimism. This work suggests that it may be best to delude ourselves by being optimistic about life's capriciousness, even though wearing rose-colored glasses might not make life rosier in reality. In a nutshell, learn to enjoy *tuche*.

We think it likely that childhood accidents are experienced to some extent similarly by siblings and that these similarities may be due to genetic factors. For adult life events there is evidence that this is the case. In one study, a standard life events measure was administered to pairs of middle-aged twins in the SATSA project described in the previous chapter. The sibling correlation for same-sex fraternal twins was significant ($r = .15$) for the total life events score, suggesting that middle-aged siblings in fact experience life events somewhat similarly. The surprise is that genetics was found to be largely responsible for sibling similarity in the frequency of life events. For the total life events measure, identical twins were twice as similar as fraternal twins. Heritability (see chapter 2) was estimated to be about 30 percent for total life events. In other words, about one-third of individual differences in the frequency of total life events is due to genetic differences between individuals.

The notion that heredity can affect life experiences is mind-boggling on first encounter, but it makes sense when we realize that what happens to us is to some extent a function of who we are—and recognize that our personality is substantially affected by heredity (see chapter 2). As we would expect from this line of reasoning, controllable life events showed greater genetic influence than uncontrollable life events. That is, the occurrence of controllable life events is related to our personalities. Nonetheless, uncontrollable events, what we would call chance, showed some genetic influence—heritability was 18 percent. In other words, as explained in chapter 2, there was greater similarity between middle-aged identical twins than between fraternal twins in the numbers of these uncontrollable events they had undergone. This must mean that such events do not occur completely by chance. Differences in the occurrence of illnesses, for example, may be the result of genetic differences in susceptibility.

This research suggests caution in assuming that chance events make siblings different—this is an empirical issue that can only be settled by studying siblings. Nonetheless, despite the surprising finding that siblings resemble each other for genetic reasons for some life events, chance is still a good bet for explaining sibling differences.

ENVIRONMENTAL EPISTASIS

Research on life events focuses on major single events. It is likely that chance also works in less heavy-handed ways. Little things, especially the concatenation of events, can link up and gently nudge development, a view of the environment that we dub *environmental epistasis*. These are Galton's "tangled strings variously twitched" by "whimsical effects of chance."

This word *epistasis* comes from genetics. It was introduced by the famous geneticist William Bateson in 1907 to describe higher-order combinations of genes that affect animals' coat color. As discussed in chapter 2, although a few single-gene effects on behavior are known, for the most part, the genetic contribution to behavioral differences among individuals involves many genes, perhaps hundreds. Each of these genes can make its own small independent contribution to variability among individuals. Genetic influence of this type is called additive because the effects of genes on behavior add up. For this reason siblings and other first-degree relatives are said to resemble each other 50 percent genetically. Our parents' genetic decks of cards are thoroughly shuffled when our hand is dealt at conception and we and each of our siblings receive a random set of half of each parent's genes. Thus, if genes that affect a behavior contribute independently—that is, if genetic effects are additive—we would resemble our parents and our siblings 50 percent for a trait that is entirely under genetic control.

However, sometimes 2 plus 2 does not equal 4—the effects of genes can be different in the presence of certain other genes. These interactive or nonindependent effects are known as epistasis. Because first-degree relatives do not have the same combination of genes, they will not resemble each other to the extent that a particular trait is affected by epistasis. The only relatives who will resemble each other for epistatic effects are identical twins, because they are identical for all combinations of genes. For this reason, the hallmark of epistatic effects is that first-degree relatives are less than half as similar as identical twins.

The genetic reshuffling that produces eggs and sperm is a random process, but the key to evolution is that this random process leads to a predictable result, that offspring resemble their parents. This occurs only to the extent that genetic effects are additive. Epistasis, on the other hand, is like genetic luck. Luck of the draw at conception can result in certain unique combinations of genes that have extraordinary effects not seen in parents or siblings. David Lykken of the University of Minnesota, who has emphasized the importance of epistasis, uses a telephone number as an example. A particular combination of seven digits makes the desired connection but a seven-digit number with any six of these numbers goes awry. Another example that Lykken uses is that of the great race horse Secretariat, who died in 1989. Secretariat was bred to many fine mares to produce hundreds of offspring. Many of Secretariat's offspring were good horses, thanks to additive genetic effects, but none came even close to the unique combination of strengths responsible for Secretariat's greatness. Epistasis is not limited to off-the-scale race horses or human geniuses. Although most genetic effects have been assumed to be additive—as they clearly are for many physical characteristics such as height—geneticists are beginning to find evidence for epistatic genetic effects for behavior within the normal range of variability. In other words, some of the differences that we see between siblings are due to genetic luck.

A more complex view of chance can be construed analogously as environmental epistasis. We drift through life in a sea full of possible environmental influences. There are some major events analogous to single-gene effects, but most effects are minor. Like additive genetic variance, many environmental perturbations affect people similarly. However, chance alignments of environmental elements can lead to unique combinations that have extraordinary effects. This is what we mean by environmental epistasis. The young boy in the Cambridge study who suffered so from the burglaries, car accidents, and the death of his grandfather could, we suggest, be seen as a victim of environmental epistasis.

A recent book by Dean Simonton of the University of California at Davis on the origins of scientific genius proposed a "chance-configuration" theory that emphasizes chance alignments (configurations) of many "mental elements" that sometimes generate scientific discoveries. Chance in this theory is inside the head, and does not refer to chance events or experiences, but its parallels with epistasis are striking.

Chaos theory is also relevant to this notion of environmental epistasis. As mentioned earlier, chaos theory attempts to find order in disorder. It is more properly described as part of the study of nonlinear (interactive and nonadditive) dynamic systems, of which weather is one of the most familiar examples. One of the key tenets that sparked the explosion of interest in chaos is *sensitive dependence on initial conditions.* In traditional linear systems, a small perturbation makes a proportionately small change in the outcome. For example, adding heat to water increases the water temperature linearly between zero degrees centigrade and 100 degrees; at those two points, however, a little difference in temperature makes a huge difference in the nature of water—a nonlinear, dynamic effect. In nonlinear systems, tiny, seemingly trivial, differences in input can lead to huge differences in output. Only half-jokingly, this has been called the "Butterfly Effect," in the sense that the flutter of a butterfly's wing in Chicago today can affect storm systems in New York next month. Chaotic systems are not predictable, but they are stable in their irregular patterns. The exact path of a leaf cannot be predicted as it floats downstream in the turbulence caused by a rock in the stream, but the seemingly random pattern of eddies that carry the leaf is a system governed by simple laws of fluid mechanics. Some events that we call chance may, like chaos, be unpredictable but orderly. Even if chaos serves as nothing more than a metaphor to remind us of the importance of nonlinear dynamic systems, it will be useful for thinking about chance.

We need to take this one step further: chance is not just being in the right place at the right time (or the wrong place at the wrong time). The impact of a constellation of events depends on the person—on his or her being the right person in the right place at the right time. Newton was not the first person to see an apple fall from a tree, but he found a new significance in this event because it slotted into his thinking about gravity (and no doubt because he was one of the brightest people who ever lived). In other words, environmental epistasis might interact with genetic epistasis.

It will be difficult to trace the effects of the chance concatenations of environmental events that we refer to as environmental epistasis, but biographies and longitudinal studies may give us opportunities to distinguish such factors in individual lives. From biographies and from isolated instances of relevant research, chance appears to be an important factor in sibling differences. Although chance is unpredictable, this does not mean that we cannot study it, or that the word is merely a label for our ignorance. We can describe many processes even though we cannot predict their occurrence. We know a lot about electrons even though Heisenberg's uncertainty principle says that there is a basic unpredictability about electrons: we can determine the speed or the position of an electron, but not both, because the act of observing one alters the other.

A start has been made towards understanding chance life events that make siblings different. It is not nothing to know that some events that look like chance are not really chance and may even depend on genetic characteristics of individuals. We need to study the role of chance in creating sibling differences, but just as important may be the role of studying siblings in helping us to understand how chance works in development. Moreover, going beyond single, major life events to consider the concatenations of minor events that we call environmental epistasis will help us understand the subtleties of the environment as it contributes to different lives within the family.

8

Implications

One thing is clear: siblings growing up in the same family are very different. It is rare in a field as complex as the behavioral sciences to discover such clear and consistent evidence for a finding that radically alters the way we think about an issue as basic as the influence of the family on development. So often we have assumed—whether we are parents, therapists, or psychologists—that the key influences on children's development are shared: their parents' personalities and childhood experiences, the quality of their parents' marriage relationship, children's educational background, the neighborhood in which they grow up, their parents' attitude to school or to discipline. The list is a very long one, but each item appears to be shared by all of the different children within a family. Yet to the extent that these influences are shared in impact, they cannot account for the differences we observe in children's outcome. And this discovery not only suggests what is wrong with our previous approaches to children's development, it also points clearly to what needs to be done: we need to find out what environmental factors make two children growing up in the same family different from one another. This is the key for unlocking the secrets of environmental influence on the development of all children, not just siblings.

The first chapter documented the vast differences between siblings in the same family, physically as well as psychologically. Chapter 2 summarized evidence from twin and adoption studies that shows, first, that genetics is responsible for the resemblance that runs in families, and, second, that genetics can explain only a small portion of the differences between siblings. Chapter 3 completed the argument concerning the importance of nonshared environment: nongenetic factors must be primarily responsible for differences between siblings. In fact, the only way that environmental influences can possibly affect the development of children's personality and psychopathology is to make siblings different, not similar. The influences from experience of this type are called *nonshared*.

The rest of the book outlined factors that might begin to answer the question of why children in the same family are so different. These factors include differential parent-child relationships, differential experiences within the sibling relationship, the impact of growing up with an individual very different from oneself, influences beyond the family, and, lastly, chance. Although it is much too early in the program of research to judge how significant each of these specific sources of nonshared environment may be for particular developmental outcomes, there are enough hints from the research reviewed in chapters 4 to 7 to predict that each of these domains makes a contribution to sibling differences. That is, the proper form of the question about the origins of individual differences is not to ask whether the major source of nonshared environmental influence is parents or siblings or environments beyond the family or chance; rather, it is to ask about the extent to which a particular outcome is affected by each of these domains, by the many components within each domain, and by combinations of them. To investigate the power of differential experiences with mother, we considered the prevalence of negative problem behavior and depressed mood in a sample of 7-year-olds. (See chapter 4.) Differences in the mothers' relationships with their two children contributed significantly to the extent of these negative outcomes. As an example of the power of differences in experience within the sibling relationship, we saw in chapter 5 that a child's self-esteem was importantly influenced by the balance of hostility given and received within the sibling relationship. It was not the "absolute" amount of hostility and criticism received from a sibling that affected children's views of themselves, but the "relative" amount: siblings who received more hostility than they gave felt worse about themselves than children who gave more than they received.

To look at these two sets of influence in this way is only the first step. The search for nonshared environmental influence is likely to be even more complicated than the exploration of the joint effects of these two sets of influence. First, we should not expect to find many simple, one-to-one associations between differential experiences of siblings and differences in outcomes. Developmental processes operate at many interacting levels, and patterns of mutual influence play a crucial role within the family. How a parent behaves to one child is, we know, linked to how that child relates to siblings. The personality and self-esteem of each child affects, and probably is affected by, each of these relationships. It is a complex network of influence, and a changing one—complex enough to frighten off all but the most foolhardy researchers, we sometimes feel! But we are beginning to be able to do more than simply lament the complexity as we piece out themes and patterns that make the detective work possible.

Second, perceptions of events and of relationships are likely to be of major significance, especially within the intense, emotional context of the family. We do not yet know much about the nature and extent of such perceptions and their role in development, but research so far suggests that the processes of influence include children's noticing and responding to the relationships, emotions, and personalities of others within the family, and comparing (privately and publicly) their own behavior and relationships with those of others.

As we described in chapters 1 and 4, writers' autobiographies reveal this sensitivity again and again: recall each of the Sitwells comparing their relationship with their mother to those of their siblings with that same (but notably different!) mother, or Mark Twain commenting on his own and his brother Henry's relationships with their mother (Tom Sawyer, Sid, and Aunt Polly). And here is Vladimir Nabokov commenting in *Speak, Memory* on his brother Sergei and himself: "I was the coddled one; he the witness of coddling." Or consider Simone de Beauvoir comparing her relationship with her parents with that of her sister Poupette:

> Relegated to a secondary position, the "little one" felt almost superfluous. I had been a new experience for my parents: my sister found it much more difficult to surprise and astonish them; I had never been compared with anyone else: she was always being compared with me.

The difference in her sister's relationships with adults with whom they were both involved, Simone saw, extended beyond the family to the world of school:

At the Cours Désir [their school] . . . whatever Poupette might do, and however well she might do it, the passing of time and the sublimation of a legend all contributed to the idea that I had done everything much better. No amount of effort and success was sufficient to break through that impenetrable barrier. The victim of some obscure malediction, she was hurt and perplexed by her situation, and often in the evening she would sit crying on her little chair. She was accused of having a sulky disposition; one more inferiority she had to put up with.

The results of systematic research tell us the same story—from Helen Koch's interviews with 5- and 6-year-olds, to our own studies of children today (chapters 4 and 5). The subjective salience of relationships within the family for each individual child is what is especially brought home to us by the research on nonshared environment. And this new emphasis on child-as-family-member meshes with the most recent evidence on the sophistication of children's social understanding within the family.

The subtlety of that understanding brings us to a third point. It is possible—even likely—that the processes of influence operate at a very subtle level. As psychologists faced with research on large numbers of persons, striving to study them by standardized methods, we inevitably reduce to clumsy categories the intricacies of relationships and the moments of insight, pressure, or excitement that shape children's lives. To simplify in this way may be to miss what matters in childrens' family lives. There is a lesson for us in our writers' understanding and exploration of lives and relationships, and of what is formative in children's experiences. We cannot of course aspire to the subtlety of Virginia Woolf's vision of the child's response to his father in *To the Lighthouse,* or Tolstoy's grasp of the shadows and happinesses of being a mother of young children, but the illumination that we gain from them should surely enlarge our own view. We need the revelation of these "epiphanies of the ordinary," to use Joyce's phrase. We may not begin to make headway in describing the nonshared experiences that matter until we begin to appreciate that subtlety.

How to make progress toward a more sensitive appreciation of what matters within the family? We will argue below for *listening* to children's and parents' views of what happens with their families—for taking the perceptions of family members very seriously, and also for conducting more naturalistic studies.

This new "nonshared" orientation toward understanding why people develop the way they do does not require us to dismiss traditional approaches to family process. Rather, it gives those notions a radically new slant, one that focuses on differences within families rather than family-by-family differences. It is from this focus that we see the implications of the nonshared environment theory for researchers, clinicians, and parents. If the effects of the environment lie in the unique world experienced by children growing up in the same family, research and therapy need to be reconceptualized, early childhood education and interventions aimed at preventing mental illness need to be rethought, and childrearing books need to be given a different slant. The importance of the theory of nonshared influence is that it implies that the specific and probably subtle differences experienced or perceived by children growing up in the same family are the environmental factors that drive the development of individual differences. These implications will be the focus of the rest of this chapter.

The argument and evidence of this book are only the beginning of a story. The surprise from which we began was that *shared* environmental influence counted for so little in the development of personality and psychopathology. The intention of the book is not to argue, however, that shared experiences are unimportant for all aspects of development. It is already clear that shared environmental influence is of major significance for some domains of children's development, most notably for cognitive development and school achievement in childhood (but not later), for physical aggression, and for aspects of delinquency. The work of Gerry Patterson and his group in Oregon has shown that there is considerable similarity between siblings in aggressive behavior, and that they and their parents "shape" each other's aggressive behavior by means of spiraling patterns of coercive interaction. For other traits we do not yet know the relative significance of shared and nonshared experiences, because they simply have not yet been studied.

Another caveat is that we do not assume that an environmental factor is either shared or nonshared. To the contrary, we assume that any particular measure of the environment can be both shared and nonshared, and that an important implication of the "nonshared" perspective is to study siblings to determine empirically the extent to which specific measures of the environment are shared or nonshared.

A final caveat concerns group differences, especially social class. In presenting colloquia on the topic of nonshared environment, we frequently encounter the following objection: How can the importance of nonshared environment be reconciled with the pervasive significance of social class in development? Siblings do after all share the social and economic background of their parents. There are a number of points to be considered in relation to group differences. Most important, average group differences rarely account for much variance. Such group differences often represent statistically significant effects that are not socially significant because variability within groups far outweighs average differences between groups. For personality and psychopathology, the focal outcomes of this book, there is little clear evidence for any class differences. For IQ, which has received most attention in class comparisons, it should be noted that the average IQ difference between siblings in the same family is 14 IQ points, whereas the average IQ difference between social classes independent of race is a mere 6 IQ points. For this reason, group differences such as social class differences have not been discussed at length. Doubtless average group differences, such as social class, could be profitably studied from a nonshared environment perspective. Nearly all research so far has assumed that an apparently shared environmental factor like social class impinges similarly on children within a family, but the effects of any such ostensibly general family factor—such as social class, discord within the family, or deprivation—can be nonshared if the factor impinges differently on different siblings because of differences in the personality, age, or expectations of the siblings. We need studies of the processes by which these apparently general factors actually impinge on children—and impinge differently for siblings within the same family.

IMPLICATIONS FOR UNDERSTANDING DEVELOPMENT

What does this new view of how experiences affect children imply for those who are concerned about understanding development? First, there is a strong message about the importance of nongenetic influences on development. It is a message that should revitalize research on environmental influences in development. The environmental research enterprise has begun to break down during the past decade—at least as far as the development of psychopathology is concerned—as it failed to produce strong, replicable results and was overtaken by the sleek new high-tech vehicles of biology. Especially in the area of mental illness, increasing acceptance of the importance of genetic influence and the promise of new genetic techniques using recombinant DNA to identify culprit genes has made it difficult to find support for research on nongenetic factors. Fifteen years ago the important message was that genetic factors affect nearly all domains of development. Today, the message is that development is by no means entirely genetically determined. Forty percent concordance for schizophrenia for identical twins is part of the coherent picture of significant and substantial genetic influence on schizophrenia, but more than half of the genetically identical pairs of twins are discordant for schizophrenia, a fact that can be explained only in terms of nongenetic influence, specifically environmental influence that is not shared. Understanding more clearly how environmental influence affects children will, then, help to restore a proper balance between research on nature and nurture.

A second general implication is that developmental research in a variety of theoretical frameworks can incorporate this new perspective with relative ease. One does not need to be "born again" as a nonshared environmental researcher to identify the specific factors responsible for making siblings growing up in a family so different from each other. The necessary studies flow naturally from any research program on development. The search for the processes by which children within the same family develop differently can be conducted within the perspective of any psychological theory—including learning, psychoanalytic, Piagetian, ethological, biopsychological, and socio-psychological theories. All are relevant and can contribute. The key is to study more than one child in each family. The vast majority of studies that compare, across families, the development of one child per family can move in the direction of uncovering nonshared influences merely by studying another child in each family. This makes it possible to ask about the extent of differences between siblings growing up in the same family, to explore the environmental sources of these sibling differences, and to search for sibling differences in environment that explain sibling differences in developmental outcomes. To reiterate the importance of taking this tack, unless environmental factors differ between siblings in the same family they cannot be important in the long run in the development of personality or psychopathology.

A third implication involves the need for measures of environmental influences that are not shared, the major factor limiting the progress of research at present. There are three ways in which measures of the environment must be improved if they are to be useful for studies of the salient nonshared experiences that affect development. First, although we have many measures of *outcome* that reveal differences between siblings, there is a need for measures of the *environment* that are sensitive to experiences that are specific to each child within a family and not shared. Because environmental research has been so imbued with the reasonable (but wrong) notion that environmental influences operate on a family-by-family basis, most measures of the family environment that have been constructed are general to the family rather than specific to the child. Obviously, items like parental education are general, and useful only in family-by-family analyses. Such general measures must be shared by siblings in a family and therefore cannot be important in the development of individual differences unless we take account of how they impinge on each child differently. Other variables which on commonsense grounds seem bound to be important, such as maternal affectionateness, are often assessed in a family-general manner ("How affectionate is mom in general towards her children?"). A measure that is general to the family in this way cannot be helpful in answering questions about nonshared influences.

Measures specific to a child ("How affectionate is mom to this particular child?") might be shared: a mother who, compared to other mothers, is particularly affectionate to one sibling might also be especially affectionate to the other sibling. We need to see empirically what happens. When we *do* look carefully, we find that there are often important differences in mothers' expressed affection (chapter 4). Through studies of siblings, measures of the environment that are specific to a child and not shared by siblings in the same family can be distinguished.

It is important to keep in mind that environmental factors that create differences within families can act independently of factors that cause differences between families, even when the same general issue is involved—parental affection, for example. Children really know only their own parents. They are unlikely to know if their parents love them more or less than other parents in other families love their children. However, they are likely to be painfully aware if their parents show them less affection than siblings. In the same way, they may know little of how their parents' discipline compares with that of other parents, but they will be acutely aware of any differences in discipline between siblings. The more we learn of children's emotions and their understanding, the clearer becomes the aptness and relevance of Charles Dickens's comments on children's perceptions of injustice, noted in chapter 4.

The significance of children's perceptions brings us to the second need for new measures. We have repeatedly noted that siblings in a family can perceive the same event differently. Children's perceptions of events are, we suggest, probably more important in relation to their development than are the "actual" events themselves. Experience is the environment as it is perceived. The difficulty of describing and assessing perceptions—especially those of children—together with a concern for scientific rigor, has pushed developmentalists to focus on the objective environment "out there" rather than on the subjective experience of environmental influences. We would argue that siblings' differential perceptions of their environments within and beyond the family are likely to prove to be an important source of the salient, nonshared influences that shape their personalities, their behavior, and their relationships.

The third need is for measures of children's active engagement, selection, and construction of their environments. Developmentalists have long since moved away from a passive model of the child as a mere receptacle for environmental influences. The case for a view of children as active builders of their own worlds, by their selection, even creation, of certain environments, and their ability to modify the impact of environments has been cogently made, from Piaget onward. But how do we measure such active "construction" of the salient world for a child? No one has made much progress here, although there are some interesting pointers in work on child language. The gap between the theoretical ideas and the practice by which they can be tested is uncomfortably large—our measures of the environment have not made the transition from the passive model to the active model of development, but it is our hunch that such active measures of the environment are more likely to capture salient sources of nonshared environment.

IMPLICATIONS FOR CLINICIANS

To many clinicians, the idea that different family members have different perceptions of what is going on in their family, different views of the meaning of other family members' behavior, is very familiar. So too is the notion that children's relationships with their siblings, their feelings about themselves, their behavior, and their self-assurance are influenced by the quality of other relationships within the family. Family systems theory in particular includes ideas that are clearly relevant to the argument for focusing upon nonshared experiences within the family: the emphasis of family systems theorists is on the unique position of each individual within subsystems of the family. A child has a unique position in the relationship with a sibling within the sibling "subsystem," and a unique position as a son or daughter within the "subsystem" of the relationship with a father. This carries the implication that siblings experience the relationships and personalities of that family differently. Family systems theorists also emphasize the importance of "feedback"; for example, a minor problem perceived by sibling B in sibling A's behavior toward B can lead to B being more hostile back to A, and A in turn becoming more hostile to B. This escalation in hostility within the sibling "subsystem" can in turn have an effect on the parents' relationship with one another—and their tension may in turn affect the two siblings. The significance of this feedback for our present argument is that it includes the idea that small differ-

163

ences in differential experience can have snowballing effects on the development of children. The attention that family theorists have paid to transitions and reorganization of subsystems within the family may be a helpful framework for thinking about significant differential experiences of siblings, as we saw in chapter 6. What then, beyond these points of agreement, does the nonshared approach to understanding development imply for clinicians?

Most important, the research conducted with a focus on nonshared environment is beginning to provide a systematic, empirical base of information on the differentiated experiences of those in the "subsystem" of siblings within the family. Family systems theory, which is more a perspective than a theory with testable hypotheses, has not been concerned with the generation of such research, but progress in the study of family influences that are not shared by siblings is relevant to family systems theorists in two ways. First, it is important in its general implications: that only through a focus on sibling differences in experience can we expose how and why individuals develop in the way that they do. Second, and more specific, it will make available information on different "subsystems" and their changing nature and influence. At present family systems theory rests primarily on case histories and provocative, illuminating examples rather than a major, systematic research base.

We have primarily considered siblings' experiences within the "normal" range of families. Family therapists, in contrast, often work with families at the extremes, such as those with abusive parents. Children's experiences in these families may be so traumatic as to overwhelm all the children within the family, with pervasive and similar effects on siblings. There is some evidence, however, that such horrors are often directed toward one child rather than distributed equally across all children in a family. We are still frustratingly ignorant about why some children are apparently less resilient than others to such stress, just as we know little about why some children are—to borrow the therapists' phrase—the "scapegoats." Systematic, rigorous study of more than a single child within such "at-risk" families could elucidate what the protective and the vulnerability factors may be.

Here lies the significance of studying nonshared experiences within the family for the majority of clinicians (who are not family systems theorists). To understand the processes leading to those differences in resilience we have to look at the microenvironment of the family for each child. For instance, to gain purchase on why and how a depressed mother affects her children, we have to be able to explain why one sibling in a family is affected while another is not. To understand the significance of a troubled marriage for the young children of that marriage, we have to be able to delineate and differentiate its impact on each child individually. The shift from a family-by-family frame of reference to an individual-by-individual perspective within the family is critical for clinicians. Clinical approaches that focus on "the enmeshed family" or that refer to "the family's sense of their experience" or "how the whole family handles worrying" cannot by themselves illuminate the development of differences between individuals. And although cures are not necessarily related to causes, it seems safe to predict that the therapeutic process will be assisted by understanding the role of nonshared environmental factors in the development of mental illness. Theories that depend on a monolithic conception of the family and which compare families as units need to be replaced with a finer-grained look at the microenvironments experienced by siblings within a family. In thinking about environmental agents that cause mental illness, we need to consider factors that can be experienced differently by two children in the same family, factors specific to each child in a family and not shared by siblings.

IMPLICATIONS FOR PARENTS

The implications of this new view of family influence do not translate into simple rules of thumb for parents, of the "all-you-have-to-do-is" variety. We are concerned here with an issue of basic science that is not yet fully understood, but some implications are clearly important. At a very general level, any clarification of what we know and do not know is valuable for parents—who have a right to whatever light psychologists can shed on the mysterious routes by which babies become people, and (perhaps even more important!) a right to know when psychologists and "experts" may have got it all wrong.

In one sense, the argument that we have outlined removes some of the blame (and credit) that parents have received in relation to the development of their children. For example, because societally important traits such as mental illness run in families, it used to be assumed that this was evidence for parental influence. But we now know (see chapter 2) that what runs in families making siblings similar is parental DNA, not parental treatment. In other words, when siblings turn out to be similar, this is more likely to be the result of their heredity than something for which their parents can be credited or blamed.

The argument for the significance of nonshared experience does of course imply that parents may have an influence on their children beyond the effects of genes that they contribute at conception; but it alters dramatically the way we think about that influence. What parents do similarly to two children—and this is often most of what the childrearing books consider in relation to parenting—cannot be important in the long run for the development of personality or problem behavior. The effects that parents may have on their children lie in the differences in the way their relationships with, their expectations of, and their attitude and behavior toward each child develops or is perceived.

Two messages for parents stand out from the ideas and evidence we have considered. One is that children are highly sensitive to differences (real or imagined) between them and their siblings in their relationships with their parents; in their parents' affection, interest, expectations, and respect; and their treatment of the different children within the family. The other is that it is such differences that are the significant influences on children's development rather than more general aspects of their parents' personality or attitudes. The research itself does not imply that parents should treat their children similarly—or differently. Such decisions involve values, and it would be inappropriate and presumptuous for us to prescribe courses of action that are so closely tied to values that will differ for different parents. But it is surely useful for parents to recognize this hypersensitivity of children to potential injustice, and to acknowledge that *differential appreciation* (to the extent it is humanly possible) is more likely to help their children than *preferential treatment*.

The first systematic studies are beginning to suggest, as we have seen, that differences in parental treatment are associated with differences in adjustment in children. A parent might well ask, however, Does this mean if I pay special attention to one child, that child will be especially well adjusted? Or does the pattern of results mean that differential treatment works only in a negative way? As researchers, we have to say immediately that we have only begun to examine these complex issues. The initial results of the Colorado study suggest the latter: parents' preferential treatment is associated with deleterious effects on the unpreferred child without increasing the adjustment or self-confidence of the preferred child.

How, though, can parents be expected to treat their children similarly when children are so different? Similar treatment will be experienced differently by these very different people; different children inevitably elicit different feelings from their parents; the match (or mismatch) of personalities in the parent-child dyad will unavoidably be different for each pair. Of course, parents can be fair about paying allowances and assigning chores, but these probably have little impact on children's development.

As parents of strikingly different children, we fully acknowledge these difficulties, and we note a further possibility: that the temperamental differences between siblings may be what underlies both the parental differentiation and the outcome differences. Consider the repeated finding that differential parental treatment is correlated with conflict between siblings. This is an association that can arise in various ways and can be interpreted in several ways in addition to the standard one that differential parental treatment causes sibling conflict. For any correlation between X and Y, one interpretation is that X causes Y, another is that Y causes X, and a third explanation is that another factor, Z, causes both X and Y. A "Z factor" may well be at work here: we believe that temperamental differences between siblings contribute both to sibling conflict and to differences in parental treatment. There is some evidence to support this unorthodox view. In a study that examined the relations between the temperament of each child, differences in parental behavior, and conflict between siblings, what turned out to be strikingly important was the *match* of the two children's personalities, rather than the particular temperament of either child considered as an individual. Conflict was much higher in those families in which the siblings differed markedly in temperament. Mismatch in temperament accounted for more of the variance in sibling conflict than either of the two children's temperaments as individuals.

In summary, the results of these first studies suggest that the aim for parents should perhaps be as far as possible to minimize the differences in their relationships with their different children, and to be especially sensitive to the acuity with which children monitor the different relationships within the family. Does the successful realization of this goal mean that parents write themselves out of their children's development? For if the effect of parents on their children is limited to differential treatment, and if parents minimize differential treatment, does it not follow that parents thereby relinquish any effect they might hope to have on their children? The answer is no. By minimizing differential treatment, parents capitalize on the biggest and best effect they could have on their children.

Are there implications for parents in the evidence for other sources of differential experience that we have discussed in the book? The results of studies of the sibling relationship suggest that children (especially those that are laterborn) who receive more negative treatment from their siblings than they mete out suffer from poor self-esteem and are less well adjusted. Parents who have to weather sibling fights and witness uneven disparagement and criticism between their children presumably scarcely need further encouragement to do their best to decrease the hostility from the "top dog" sibling. Our evidence provides yet more reason to do so. The research has gone further, suggesting some guidelines for parents, at least of young siblings, about how to smooth things out.

The evidence on differences between siblings in their experiences outside the family is, as we saw in chapter 6, extremely sparse. It seems a strong possibility that peer groups differ substantially for children within the same family. For parents who are concerned about one child's group of friends, it is worth noting that parents' monitoring of adolescents' activities with peers—keeping track of who they are with and where they go—is associated with the children exhibiting fewer problems. Finally there are the effects of chance, outlined in chapter 7, which possibly contribute to different developmental trajectories for siblings. By definition it would be difficult for a parent to protect a child from unfortunate chance events with a negative impact, but there is perhaps a lesson in the idea of cumulative impact—the notion of "environmental epistasis" we discussed. For some children particularly, who are perhaps initially more vulnerable, there can be a downward spiral of events into severe trouble: recall the boy who suffered increasingly from a series of car accidents, burglaries, and so on, or the girl who on moving house had difficulties at school that set off further problems. Parents who can keep a "weather eye" open for the effects of initial squalls may manage to protect such vulnerable children from the steepest downward spirals.

Parents with single children often ask how this emphasis on differentiation between siblings applies to them. And what are the implications for first-time parents? Understanding how specific experiences that are not shared affect singleton children is important for appreciating the wider significance of the theory. It is not just a theory of sibling differences. Rather, the theory uses differences between siblings as the key to understanding how the environment affects the development of all children, singletons as well as siblings. The general theme is that the macroenvironments of families that would affect all children in the family similarly are not important for children's development. We argue that parental education and occupation per se do not matter. What is important is the microenvironment within the family, things that can be experienced differently by two children growing up in the same family. For example, if, as appears to be the case, differential parental affection influences children's later self-esteem, this means that parents' affection specific to one child—not parents' general affectionateness—affects children's development. This could affect the development of self-esteem of a singleton child as well as a sibling child. The difference is that singleton children are not affected by the contrasts and interactions with siblings. Other themes stand out as equally relevant for parents of singletons and those with siblings. The theory draws attention to children's sensitivity and responsiveness to other relationships within the family, to the significance—even for very young children—of relative appreciation and deprivation, and the salience of comparison processes. The message is relevant for all parents, that children are acutely sensitive to their place in the network of family relationships.

In closing, we suggest that the implications of nonshared environment extend beyond our roles as researchers, clinicians, and parents: it is a theory of who we are and how we got to be the way we are. In order to understand ourselves as well as our children and clients, we need to think about the differences between us and our siblings, the separate lives we lead within our own families.

SEPARATE LIVES

A life is not the mere growth of the original seed. It runs the continual danger of being halted, broken, damaged or turned aside. Yet a happy beginning does encourage the subject to get the best that can be got from his circumstances. . . . A comparison of my fate with my sister's is very revealing: her road was far harder than mine. . . . In the photographs that were taken of me at two and a half I have a determined and self-confident expression; hers at the same age show a frightened, timid look. . . . It took her a long time to make a complete break with her childhood. Mine was calm and happy. . . .

She helped me to assert myself . . . I believe I should count the fact of having had a sister, younger than myself but close to me in age, as one of my pieces of good luck.

—Simone de Beauvoir, *All Said and Done*

Notes

(See References for full bibliographic data on works cited.)

PROLOGUE

P. ix David Lodge should be required reading for academics who need to laugh more: *Changing places* (1979), *Small world* (1984), and his latest, *Nice work* (1989).

P. x Behavioral genetics and its methods are described in chapter 2. The notes for chapter 2 include references for further reading in this area.

P. x Quotation from Francis Galton: Galton (1875, p. 576). Quotation from Charles Darwin: Darwin (1958, p. 43).

P. xi Reference for Jensen: Jensen (1969).

P. xi Reference to book on siblings: Dunn and Kendrick (1982).

P. xi Reference to Solomon Diamond: Diamond (1957).

P. xii Reference to book on temperament: Buss and Plomin (1975).

P. xiii Reference to proceedings of CIBA conference on temperament: Porter and Collins (1982).

NOTES

CHAPTER 1

Autobiographical and Biographical References

P. 1 Leon Edel, the distinguished biographer of Henry James, notes that "Autobiography is written out of experience, memory, emotion; biography is a re-living and re-examination of someone else's experience, and this distinction had to be borne in mind constantly" (Edel 1953, p. 345). For our purposes both the autobiographical memories and the biographer's reexaminations are relevant. We refer to only a few of the sometimes large number of works on our subjects; we have selected those biographies that are themselves exceptional pieces of writing, in which the task of reexamination of the subject's life has been carried out in a particularly penetrating manner.

P. 1 Mark Twain: Twain (1966). Quotations concerning Henry/Sid: Twain (1966, pp. 35, 36, 100).

P. 2 Henry James and siblings: James (1913, 1914), Edel (1953). Quotations from James: (1913, p. 2) and (1914, p. 151). Note Henry's comparison of himself to his younger brother Wilky, who was greatly at ease with others:

> my brother Wilky . . . contrived in those years to live . . . with an immediacy that left me far in the lurch. I was always still wondering how, while he had solved the question simply *ambulando*, which was for him but by the merest sociable stroll. This represented to me success—success of a kind, but of such an assured kind—in a degree that was my despair. (James 1914, p. 33.)

William James makes a similar comparison in the letter to his parents quoted above, referring to Henry as "less fatal than the light fantastic and ever-sociable Wilky." (James 1914, p. 151).

P. 3 A.E. and Laurence Housman: see Maas's (1972) edition of the *Letters of A. E. Housman;* Housman (1969). Quotation: Maas (1972, p. 4).

P. 5 John Keats: Gittings (1968).

P. 5 Shelley: Holmes (1976). Quotation from Hellen Shelley: Hogg (1858, p. 23), as quoted in Holmes (1976).

P. 6 The Brontë siblings: Gerin (1967), Gaskell ([1857] 1975).

P. 6 Proust: Painter (1959).

P. 6 Leo Tolstoy, his siblings, and the quotation from the Tolstoys' tutor: Troyat (1970). See also Tolstoy ([1852] 1964) for portrait of Nicholas.

P. 6 Thomas and Heinrich Mann: Hamilton (1978, 1983), Mann (1918).

NOTES

P. 7 George Eliot: Eliot ([1860] 1979), Haight (1968). D. H. Lawrence: Callow (1975), Lawrence ([1913] 1981), Nehls (1957). Virginia Woolf: Bell (1972), Woolf (1975). Katherine Mansfield ([1916] 1954). Rudyard Kipling: Wilson (1978). Oscar Wilde: Ellmann (1988). Lewis Carroll: Clark (1979).

Height and Weight Data

P. 8 Galton's data on height and weight as well as his behavioral data presented later in the chapter were derived from Galton (1889) and a reanalysis of these data (Johnson et al. 1985). The behavioral data are based on a sample of 279 pairs of brothers and 105 pairs of sisters. Average differences between siblings were obtained using the following relationship between correlations (r) and average differences: $1.13 \ \sigma\sqrt{1-r}$ with standard deviations ($[\sigma]$) derived from Galton's data.

Correlation

P. 9 Over a hundred years ago in England, Galton faced the problem of describing familial resemblance for the diameter of pea seeds. Galton solved the problem, which he called co-relation, and his famous student, Karl Pearson, provided the finishing touches. The statistic, now known as the Pearson product-moment correlation coefficient, is the basis for describing associations between pairs of things, not just family members, in all of science.

Galton realized that average differences were not very useful because their interpretation depends upon the extent of differences in the population. For example, the average sibling difference of 1.5 inches in height makes more sense when you know that the average difference between persons picked randomly two at a time from the population is 2.25 inches. In other words, we need to express average sibling differences in terms of differences in the population. Another problem with average difference scores is that we cannot compare resemblance for different variables because they are measured on different scales. For example, the average sibling difference for height is 1.5 inches, while for weight it is 20 pounds.

The essence of Galton's solution was to express each individual's score as a deviation from the average score of all individuals. Pair resemblance is assessed by covariance which is calculated by multiplying one sibling's devia-

175

tion from the population average by the other sibling's deviation. Covariance is the average of these products across all sibling pairs. For example, if one sibling is above average in height and so is the other, the product of the positive deviations of the two siblings contributes positively to sibling covariance for height. Variance describes differences among individuals in a population by multiplying each individual's deviation from the population average by itself. Variance is the average of these squared deviations. A correlation is the ratio of the covariance to the variance, that is, the extent to which variance in the population covaries within pairs of siblings. Thus the correlation between siblings for height is .50, because sibling covariance for height is 2 and the variance is 4.

Correlation and Variance

P. 10 Readers familiar with statistics know that correlations are usually squared to estimate variance explained. Why does the sibling correlation of .5 for height mean that 50 percent of the variance in height is due to sibling resemblance (i.e., to covariance)? Squaring the correlation would suggest that only 25 percent of the variance in height is explained. The answer is that in the case of the sibling correlation, we are trying to describe the proportion of the variance in the population that is due to sibling resemblance. This is the sibling correlation itself, not the squared correlation. As explained above, the correlation represents the ratio of sibling covariance to population variance. Correlations are squared when we want to know how much of the variance of one sibling's score can be predicted by scores of the other member of the sibling pairs. For example, if we wanted to know how much of the variance of one sibling's height can be predicted by the other sibling's height, the answer lies in the squared correlation. The correlation itself, however, indicates how much of the variance in height covaries for siblings. In this book, we focus on 1.0 minus the correlation as an index of how different siblings are.

Physical Traits and Disease

P. 10 Sibling correlations for facial characteristics: Susanne (1975); other physical characteristics: Cohen et al. (1973), Nichols and Bilbro (1966);

NOTES

disease: Edforst-Lubs (1971), Holm, Hauge, and Jensen (1982), Kendler and Robinette (1983).

Qualitative Traits and the Phi Coefficient

P. 11 For either-or traits, such as most diseases, sibling data are usually reported as concordance, the percentage of pairs in which both members contract the disease. As discussed in the text, the problem with sibling concordance is that it needs to be compared with the incidence of the disease in the population. A special type of correlation called phi incorporates the population incidence and sibling concordance for either-or traits (Guilford and Fruchter 1973). The phi coefficient can be interpreted much like the usual Pearson product-moment correlation. Researchers often compute "liability correlations" which assume that a continuous distribution underlies such either-or traits (Smith 1974). Many assumptions are made when sibling correlations are estimated for a hypothetical liability rather than for the actual categorical data; we prefer to report the phi coefficient, because it stays closer to the data and can be more readily interpreted in terms of sibling differences.

Sibling Difference as 1.0 Minus Sibling Correlation

P. 12 In tables 1.1 and 1.2, sibling differences are calculated as 1.0 minus the sibling correlation. As explained above, the sibling correlation denotes the proportion of variance that covaries for siblings. 1.0 minus the sibling correlation estimates variance that is not shared by siblings. For either-or disease states, sibling concordance has been converted to the phi coefficient using population incidence estimates. The phi coefficient has been treated in the same way as the sibling correlation to represent the extent of sibling differences.

Psychological Traits

P. 12–20 Quote from Galton (1892, p. 314). IQ reference: Bouchard and McGue (1981). Study of adult sibling IQ: DeFries et al. (1979). Specific mental abilities: DeFries, Vandenberg, and McClearn (1976); DeFries et al. (1979); Plomin (1988). School achievement and a review of other psychological domains: Plomin (1986). Reading disability: Stevenson et al. (1987); Finnuci and Childs, (1983). Mental retardation: Johnson, Ahern, and Johnson (1976); Nichols (1984). Alzheimer's disease: Heston and Mastri (1977). Personality: Ahern et al. (1982); Loehlin, Willerman, and Horn (1988); Plomin (1986). Schizophrenia: Gottesman and Shields (1982). Affective disorders: Reich et al. (1987); Rice et al. (1987); McGuffin and Katz (1986). Delinquency: Gottesman, Carey, and Hanson (1983); Rowe (1986). Criminality: Wilson and Herrnstein (1985); Mednick, Moffit, and Stack (1987). Alcoholism: Cotton (1979). Quotation from Scarr: Scarr and Grajek (1982, p. 361).

CHAPTER 2

Autobiographical and Biographical References

P. 21 Quotation concerning the Huxley brothers: West (1983, p. 167). Reference to Joyce: Kimball (1983); quotation from Stanislaus Joyce and Svevo reference to the Joyce brothers as Don Quixote and Sancho Panza: Joyce (1958). For K. Mansfield and D. H. Lawrence material, see notes to chapter 1.

Genetics

P. 22 Many excellent texts describe Mendelian genetics and the molecular genetic mechanisms that underlie hereditary transmission from one generation to the next. We do not describe the molecular genetic underpinnings of heredity because it is not necessary to know them in order to understand the genetic causes of sibling differences. A lively account of the discovery of DNA structure and function has been written by one of its discoverers, James Watson (1968). With John Tooze, Watson (1981) has also written a highly readable account of the recombinant DNA techniques used so widely in modern molecular genetic research.

P. 12 Mendel's classic 1866 paper is well worth reading and is available in translation in many genetics texts. Fisher's 1918 paper on the expected resemblance of relatives is also highly recommended. The classic text on

NOTES

quantitative genetics with a focus on animal breeding is D. S. Falconer (1989). A general reference for Mendelian genetics, quantitative genetic methods, and molecular genetics as they relate to the study of behavior is Plomin, DeFries, and McClearn (1990). For an excellent compendium of both animal and human behavioral genetic research, including more than a thousand references, see Fuller and Thompson (1978). For a review of the human behavioral genetics literature on cognitive abilities, personality, and psychopathology from a developmental perspective, see Plomin (1986). More selective reviews include Dixon and Johnson (1980) and Plomin (1990). The *Annual Review of Psychology* included chapters reviewing recent developments in behavioral genetics in 1960, 1966, 1971, 1974, 1978, 1982, 1985, and 1988; the 1991 chapter is in press (Plomin and Rende, in press). *Behavior Genetics,* a bimonthly journal published since 1970, is a major repository of animal and human behavioral genetic research.

P. 27 A discussion of the mania followed by depression in the reports of linkage for psychopathology can be found in Plomin (1990), which also contains references for the failures to replicate these linkages. References for linkages to single-gene disorders are included in Plomin, DeFries, and McClearn (1990).

P. 29 Evidence for nonadditive genetic effects on personality and psychopathology is considered by Plomin, Chipuer, and Loehlin (in press) and by Plomin, Rende, and Rutter (in press).

Calculating Heritability

P. 32 Whenever a statistically significant effect is found, the next question concerns the size of the effect. Many statistically significant effects are not in practice significant, because they account for so little of the variance. In the case of genetics, we can also ask about effect size, and when we do, the answer often is that genetic effects are not only significant, they are also substantial.

Heritability is a statistic that indicates the proportion of a trait's variance due to genetic differences among individuals. As described in the notes for chapter 1, a correlation is a statistic that ascribes the proportion of trait variance due to covariance. In the case of identical twins adopted apart in uncorrelated environments, their correlation represents the proportion of phenotypic variance that is due to genetic variance that covaries between the members of the identical twin pairs. Identical twins adopted apart covary only for genetic reasons if they were reared apart in uncorrelated environments. Thus, the correlation for identical twins reared apart directly estimates heritability. In the case of adopted-apart first-degree relatives, their correlation represents the proportion of phenotypic variance that is due to half the genetic variance, because first-degree relatives are only 50 percent similar genetically. Thus, their correlation estimates half of the heritability; doubling the correlation estimates heritability.

The same logic applies to more complicated designs, such as the twin method, that depend on the difference between correlations for different groups. Doubling the difference between correlations for identical and fraternal twins reared together estimates heritability for the following reason. For twins reared together, the covariance for identical twins includes all genetic influence plus shared environment. The covariance for fraternal twins also includes shared environment, but only half the genetic influence. Thus, the difference between the two correlations estimates half the heritability and doubling the difference estimates heritability.

Reasonably accurate estimates of heritability require large sample sizes. It cannot be overemphasized that heritability is a descriptive statistic that refers to the extent to which genetic differences among individuals in a particular population account for observed differences given that population's mix of genetic and environmental influences as they exist at that time. Heritability is not a constant and it does not imply fixed, immutable effects of genes. More detailed discussion of the estimation and interpretation of heritability can be found in Plomin, DeFries, and McClearn (1990).

Evidence for Genetic Influence

P. 33 Physical characteristics. Height and weight: Plomin (1986). Facial characteristics: Susanne (1975).

P. 35 Common diseases. Cancers: Holm, Hauge, and Jensen (1982). Eczema, asthma, and hay fever: Edforst-Lubs (1971). Heart disease, ulcers, diabetes, and hypertension: Kendler and Robinette (1983).

P. 36 Psychological traits. For a general discussion of research on intelligence, including a review of behavioral genetic research, see Vernon (1979). The summary of behavioral genetic research on IQ by Bouchard and McGue

NOTES

(1981) was used to estimate genetic influence. For other psychological traits, reviews of behavioral genetic results by Plomin (1986) and Plomin, DeFries, and McClearn (1990) were used to estimate genetic influence.

CHAPTER 3

Between-Family Environmental Influences

P. 42 Maccoby and Martin (1983) and Wachs and Gruen (1982) review traditional between-family research on the association between family environment and children's development; Maccoby and Martin emphasize that relatively little of the variance in individual outcomes can be explained by traditional "between-family" comparisons.

It should be noted that between-family studies are not the same as studies of shared environment. That is, between-family research examines a particular aspect of the family and one child's outcome in the family and correlates these across families. The measure of the family environment could be shared or nonshared—this issue cannot be resolved until we study more than one child per family.

The Importance of Nonshared Environment

P. 43 Although researchers in behavioral genetics have for decades mentioned that their results imply that most environmental influences are of the nonshared variety, the first lengthy discussion of the importance of nonshared environment was Loehlin and Nichols (1976). Rowe and Plomin (1981) first focused on the importance of nonshared environment and gave it its name. For the real debut of the topic, which appeared with thirty-two commentaries and a response to the commentaries, see Plomin and Daniels (1987). We encourage readers to examine these commentaries to assess for themselves the adequacy of the claim of the importance of nonshared environment.

P. 44 For reviews of recent studies of adoptive siblings as well as other data that converge on the conclusion that most environmental influence is of the nonshared variety, see Plomin and Daniels (1987) and Plomin, DeFries, and McClearn (1990). Reviews of the importance of nonshared environment for specific domains are also available: schizophrenia (Gottesman and Shields, 1982); juvenile delinquency and criminality (Plomin, Nitz, and Rowe, 1989); IQ and specific cognitive abilities (Plomin, 1988).

P. 52 Twin study of IQ for children living in kibbutzim: Nathan and Guttman (1984); meta-analysis of twin studies of IQ showing that the importance of shared environment declines through the life course: McCartney, Harris, and Bernieri (1990).

P. 54 For descriptions of elephant family relationships, see Moss (1988).

P. 54 Inbred mice are described in greater detail in Plomin et al. (1990); for a report on nonshared environment in mice, see Neiderhiser and Plomin (1990).

Error of Measurement

P. 56 Nongenetic sibling differences include errors of measurement as well as nonshared environment. We have not emphasized this distinction for two reasons. First, the measures that we described are reasonably reliable—typically reliability estimates are .80 to .90. This means that 10 percent to 20 percent of the total variance may be due to error of measurement. This variance has been counted as nonshared environment. Thus, nonshared environment independent of unreliability may be reduced from 50 percent to 40 percent or even 30 percent. However, this does not alter our main conclusion that nonshared environment accounts for a substantial amount of variance. Second, short-term inconsistencies in response that we call error may be due to systematic changes in state that involve nonshared environment rather than error (Plomin and Nesselroade, 1990).

CHAPTER 4

Autobiographical and Biographical References

P. 60 Katherine Mansfield: Tomalin (1988); quotation from her *Journal:* Mansfield ([1937] 1954).

NOTES

P. 61 Glendinning (1981) gives details of incidents perceived differently by the Sitwell siblings. Sitwell autobiographies: E. Sitwell (1965), O. Sitwell (1944, 1946), S. Sitwell (1943).

What Do Siblings Say?

P. 62 Mary Wollstonecraft, see Tomalin (1974).

P. 62 For both Mansfield and Wollstonecraft a persuasive argument can be made for parent partiality for the other siblings as central to the women's intellectual and emotional drive. For D. H. Lawrence the impact of differential maternal affection within the family was, according to his biographers, complex and changing, but profound, as the evidence of his own account in *Sons and Lovers* surely makes clear. See Callow (1975).

P. 60–62 While Edith Sitwell and Mansfield both adored their brothers despite parental partiality, for many others parental partiality was connected to a strong antipathy for the favored sibling. The great French writer Stendhal recalls his father's partiality for his second sister Zenaide in his autobiographical *Life of Henri Brulard* (1958) and his own response to the favored treatment that she received:

> I detested my younger sister Zenaide because my father made a pet of her and would lull her to sleep on his knees every evening, and because she was loudly championed by Mlle Seraphie [Stendhal's aunt]. I covered the plasterwork in the house (coated with whitewash) with caricatures of Zenaide the *telltale*. My sister Pauline and I accused Zenaide of spying on us, and I believe we weren't far wrong.

P. 62–63 For Helen Koch's pioneering studies, see Koch (1960). For evidence on children's jealousy of father, see Dunn and Kendrick (1982).

P. 64 For the study of a nationally representative sample of siblings, see Daniels et al. (1985). The SIDE was developed by Daniels and Plomin (1985) and used in studies by Anderson (1989), Baker and Daniels (in press), Daniels (1986), and Daniels and Plomin (1985).

What Do Siblings Do?

P. 68 The Cambridge studies include a longitudinal study of firstborn children followed from before the birth of their sibling through the infancy of the secondborn (Dunn and Kendrick 1982); a longitudinal study of families (the Cambridge Sibling Study) which focused on the secondborn children and their older siblings, studied when the secondborn children were 18 months, 2 years, 3 years, and 6 years (Dunn and Munn 1985); a detailed study of secondborn children observed with their siblings and mothers at 14, 16, 18, 20, and 24 months (see Dunn 1988; Dunn and Munn 1985); and a detailed study of secondborn children at 24, 26, 28, 30, 33, and 36 months. (Dunn and Shatz, 1989).

P. 68 The observations of firstborn children's reaction to interaction between mother and baby sibling are reported in Dunn and Kendrick (1982). For the analysis of children's interventions in conversations, see Dunn and Shatz (1989).

What Do Parents Say?

P. 74 Quotation concerning Mary James: Edel (1953) p.68.

The Colorado study of siblings is part of the Colorado Adoption Project (Plomin, DeFries, and Fulker 1988). For the report on maternal differential treatment in that study, see Stocker, Dunn, and Plomin (1989). The same maternal interview was employed in the Cambridge Sibling Study (see Dunn and Stocker 1989) when the secondborn were 6 years old. Note that parents of adolescent siblings in the nationally representative sample reported by Daniels et al. (1985) were more likely to say they treated their children similarly, a clear-cut difference with their own children's views reported earlier. It is not clear whether this difference between the data from the Colorado and Cambridge studies is a reflection of age differences in the children in the families studied or in the interview techniques used. (More intensive, intimate, probing, and detailed interviews were used in the Colorado and Cambridge studies.)

Should We Take Interviews Seriously?

P. 75 Quotation from Henry James on the importance of perceptions: Edel (1987) p.1.

P. 76–77 Quotations from mothers concerning feelings toward firstborn following birth of the second child and toward secondborn: Dunn and

NOTES

Kendrick (1982). For evidence on the agreement between maternal interview and direct observation, see Dunn and Kendrick (1982).

To What Extent Do Parents Behave Differentially to Their Children?

P. 77 For description and analysis of parental differential treatment in the Colorado Adoption Project, see Stocker, Dunn, and Plomin (1989). Data on the Cambridge sample comes from the Cambridge Sibling Study, which employed the same maternal interview.

P. 77 Quotation from Sandra Scarr: Scarr (1987).

P. 78 The evidence on maternal behavior when each sibling was the same age is reported in Dunn, Plomin, and Daniels (1986); Dunn, Plomin, and Nettles (1985); and Dunn and Plomin (1986).

P. 78–79 Note that not all parents are equally consistent towards their different children at similar ages. The Colorado study showed there is a large range of differences between mothers in the extent to which they are consistent, with some mothers being very affectionate to particular children, or showing more controlling and restrictive behavior to one child in the family. We explored this range of differences between mothers and found that the extent to which a mother showed consistency in her behavior to her two children when they were the same age was related to her personality, her IQ, her age, and her education. The more extraverted, sociable mothers tended to interact more similarly with their two children than the more anxious, nervous, and easily upset mothers. The more educated mothers also tended to treat their children with more differentiation (Dunn and Plomin 1986).

Links to Outcome

P. 80 Charles Dickens: Hibbert (1967) and Kaplan (1988); for autobiographical material see Forster (1903).

P. 81 The national sample study is Daniels et al. (1985). The other studies referred to in this section are Baker and Daniels (1990), Daniels (1986), and Daniels et al. (1985). The relation between adjustment and differential treatment in the Colorado study is reported in Dunn, Stocker, and Plomin (1990), and self-esteem and sibling behavior in Dunn, Stocker, and Beardsall (1989).

185

NOTES

Parental Differentiation as a Response to Differences Between Siblings

P. 83 For the Cambridge results on self-esteem and differential treatment, see Dunn, Stocker, and Beardsall (1989). The study of identical twins is Baker and Daniels (in press), and the study of adoptive and nonadoptive siblings is Daniels and Plomin (1985). The study of elderly parents' favoritism is Aldous, Klaus, and Klein (1985).

Birth Order

P. 85 For overview of birth order findings, see Ernst and Angst (1983); see also Schooler (1972).

CHAPTER 5

P. 88–89 For discussion of and research on the separate contributions of two partners to a dyadic relationship, see Hinde (1979).

Autobiographical and Biographical References

P. 88 Quotation from Nancy and Carl: Cambridge Sibling Study.

P. 89 For discussion of "two marriages," see Bernard (1982).

P. 90 For George Eliot's childhood relationship with her brother Isaac, see her sonnet "Brother and Sister" (Eliot 1888) and Haight (1968).

P. 92 Biographical and autobiographical evidence on sibling differences in leadership and dominance: Tolstoy: Troyat (1970), Wilson (1988). Quotation from Laurence Housman: Housman (1969, p. 22). Quotation from Anthony Trollope: Trollope ([1947] 1978, p. 7). William James's criticism of Henry: Edel (1987, p. 65). Chekhov letters: Yarolinsky (1974). Keats's letters: Keats (1935). Quotation from Stanislaus Joyce: Joyce (1958, p. 17).

Research on Differences in Sibling Relationships

P. 89 For one example of research delineating different dimensions of the dyadic relationship between siblings, see Furman and Buhrmester (1985).

P. 93 For research demonstrating the effects of being a teacher and being

NOTES

a pupil in peer interactions, see Damon and Phelps (1989); Doise and Mugny (1984); and Glachan and Light (1982). See also Piaget (1959 and [1932] 1965).

P. 97 For studies using the SIDE, see Anderson (1989), Baker and Daniels (1990), Daniels (1986), and Daniels and Plomin (1985).

P. 102 Cambridge study: Dunn and Stocker (1989). The Colorado Adoption Project study: Dunn and Plomin (1986). Study of siblings in dual-earner families: Stocker and McHale (1989).

P. 108 The Colorado study reporting links between differential sibling experiences and outcomes is Dunn, Stocker and Plomin (1990). The observations of differential sibling behavior come from the Colorado and Cambridge studies.

P. 109 Evidence for the early developing interest in social comparison within the family can be found in Dunn (1988).

P. 110 Quotations from firstborn children (Bruce S. and Laura W.): Dunn and Kendrick (1982); the quotation from Johnny, Sarah, and their mother comes from the Pennsylvania Sibling Study, which is ongoing. For the study on reactions of children to disputes between their older siblings and their mothers, see Dunn and Munn (1985). For the study of questions about others' feelings, see Dunn (1988).

CHAPTER 6

Autobiographical and Biographical References

P. 116 Goethe's relationship with his sister: Friedenthal (1965) and Read (1984). See references for Dickens, Kipling, and Eliot in notes for previous chapters. For the inference that Alice James was not affected by the timing of the European experience see Edel (1964, p. 4).

Peers

P. 118 For a recent discussion of the developmental significance of peer relationships, see Berndt and Ladd (1988). See also Piaget ([1932] 1965). For studies of peers and deviance, and role of siblings and other family factors, see Brook, Nomura, and Cohen (1988) and Brook et al. (1989). For evidence on peers and adjustment, see Parker and Asher (1987).

P. 119 For studies using the SIDE, see Anderson (1989), Baker and Daniels (in press), Daniels (1986), and Daniels and Plomin (1985).

Life-Span Studies

P. 125 The life-span perspective on development has been promulgated by a group of theorists and researchers, most notably Paul Baltes. This approach and the specific predictions described in the test can be found in Baltes, Reese, and Lipsitt (1980). See also Hetherington, Lerner, and Perlmutter (1988).

P. 126–28 The study of women who were brought up in institutions is summarized in Quinton and Rutter (1988). For empirical studies of transition points during the life course and personality, see Caspi, Elder, and Bem (1987, 1988).

P. 129 The example of sibling differences in response to a house move comes from the Cambridge Sibling Study (Beardsall and Dunn 1989).

P. 130 For a discussion of behavioral genetics from a life-span perspective, see Plomin and Thompson (1987); for an overview of behavioral genetics and aging, see Plomin and McClearn (1990).

P. 130 For an overview of the Swedish Adoption/Twin Study of Aging (SATSA), see Pedersen et al. (in press) and Plomin and McClearn (1990). For major reports of SATSA personality results, see Pedersen et al. (1988) and Plomin et al. (1988). A study of Finnish twins reared together concludes that adult correlated environments (such as degree of contact) are associated with personality (Rose et al. 1988), although the results are difficult to interpret because it is possible that more similar twins are in greater contact.

CHAPTER 7

P. 135 Quotations from Simone de Beauvoir: de Beauvoir (1977).

P. 135 Quotations from Galton: Galton (1889, pp. 21, 195).

P. 137 For a thorough discussion of the role of chance in the history of philosophy, see Nussbaum (1986).

P. 138 Quotation from Darwin: Darwin (1892, p. 28).

NOTES

P. 138 Reference for François Jacob: Jacob (1988).

P. 139 Quotation about Kipling: Wilson (1978). For references to the biographical and autobiographical material on Kipling and Henry James, see the notes to previous chapters. For the discussion of Virginia Woolf's intellectual "transformation," see Bell (1972).

P. 141 Reference on life events: Holmes and Rahe (1967); for a balanced review of this research, which raises the distinction between controllable and uncontrollable life events, see Thoits (1983). For the Cambridge research on life events and young siblings, see Beardsall and Dunn (1989). For the twin study of life events, see Plomin et al. (1990).

P. 144 For a new book on learned helplessness by one of the founders of the field, see Seligman (in press). For a discussion of self-deception as a source of mental health, productivity, and persistence, see Taylor (1989).

P. 145 Reference to genetic epistasis: Lykken (1982). For an overview of the evidence in favor of nonadditive genetic effects for personality, see Plomin, Chipuer, and Loehlin (in press). The Oxford English Dictionary traces the first use of *epistasis* to William Bateson in 1907.

P. 148 Reference for Simonton: Simonton (1989). For recent discussions of the role of chance in scientific discovery, see Root-Bernstein (1989), Kohn (1989), and Roberts (1989).

P. 148 *Chaos: Making a new science* (Gleick 1987) is a beautifully written book.

CHAPTER 8

P. 154 Quotation from Vladimir Nabokov: Nabokov ([1947] 1989); quotations from Simone de Beauvoir: de Beauvoir (1963, p. 42).

P. 157 For the approach of Patterson and his research group, see Patterson (1982, 1986).

P. 158 For details concerning average IQ differences between siblings, see Plomin and DeFries (1980); for a discussion of average IQ differences between social classes, see Jensen (1980).

P. 162 For child language research that addresses the problem of documenting children's active role in constructing environment, see Shatz (1987).

P. 163 For a discussion of the relations between family systems theory and developmental psychologists' approaches to child development, see Minuchin (1985). For a discussion of the foundations of family therapy, see Hoffman (1981).

P. 167 For evidence on the relations between negative problem behavior and differential experiences with parents, see Dunn, Stocker, and Plomin (1990).

P. 167 For a discussion of sibling relationships aimed at a general audience, see Dunn (1985).

P. 169 For the study showing mismatch between siblings in temperament related to the frequency of conflict between them, see Munn and Dunn (1989).

P. 169 For discussion of the implications of research on young siblings for parental practices, see Dunn (1984) and Dunn and Kendrick (1982).

P. 172 Quotation from Simone de Beauvoir, see de Beauvoir (1977) pp. 12–13, 15.

References

AHERN, F. M., JOHNSON, R. C., WILSON, J. R., McCLEARN, G. E., AND
VANDENBERG, S. G. 1982. Family resemblances in personality. *Behavior
Genetics* 12: 261–80.

ALDOUS, J., KLAUS, E., AND KLEIN, D. M. 1985. The understanding heart:
Aging parents and their favorite children. *Child Development* 56: 303–
16.

ANDERSON, S. L. 1989. Differential within-family experiences as predictors
of adolescent personality and attachment style differences. Honors thesis,
Department of Psychology, Harvard University.

BAKER, L. A., AND DANIELS, D. 1990. Nonshared environmental influences
and personality differences in adult twins. *Journal of Personality and
Social Psychology* 58:103–110.

BALTES, P. B., REESE, H. W., AND LIPSITT, L. P. 1980. Life-span developmental psychology. *Annual Review of Psychology* 31: 65–110.

BEARDSALL, L., AND DUNN, J. 1989. Life events in childhood: Shared and
nonshared experiences of siblings. Manuscript.

BECKSON, K. 1983. The importance of being angry: The mutual antagonism
of Oscar and Willie Wilde. In *Blood brothers: Siblings as writers,* ed. N.
Kiell. New York: International Universities Press.

BELL, Q. 1972. *Virginia Woolf.* Vol. 1. London: Hogarth Press.

BERNARD, J. S. 1982. *The future of marriage.* New Haven: Yale University
Press.

BERNDT, T. J., AND LADD, G. W. 1989. *Peer relationships in child development.* New York: Wiley.

REFERENCES

BOUCHARD, T. J., JR., AND MCGUE, M. 1981. Familial studies of intelligence: A review. *Science* 212: 1055–59.

BROOK, J. S., NOMURA, C., AND COHEN, P. 1989. A network of influences on adolescent drug involvement: Neighborhood, school, peer, and family. *Genetic, Social and General Psychology Monographs* 115: 123–45.

BROOK, J. S., WHITEMAN, M., GORDON, A. S., AND BROOK, D. W. 1989. The role of older brothers in younger brothers' drug use viewed in the context of parent and peer influences. Manuscript.

BUSS, A. H., AND PLOMIN, R. 1975. *A temperament theory of personality development.* New York: Wiley-Interscience.

CALLOW, P. 1975. *Son and lover: The young Lawrence.* London: The Bodley Head.

CANNON, W. B. 1940. The role of chance in discovery. *Scientific Monthly* 50: 204–9.

CASPI, A., ELDER, G. H., AND BEM, D. J. 1987. Moving against the world: Life-course patterns of explosive children. *Developmental Psychology* 23: 308–13.

CASPI, A., ELDER, G. H., AND BEM, D. J. 1988. Moving away from the world: Life-course patterns of shy children. *Developmental Psychology* 24: 824–31.

CHEKHOV, A. 1974. *Letters of Anton Chekhov,* ed. A. Yarmolinsky. London: Jonathan Cape.

CLARK, A. 1979. *Lewis Carroll: A biography.* London: J. M. Dent.

COHEN, D. J., DIBBLE, E., GRAWE, J. M., AND POLLIN, W. 1973. Separating identical from fraternal twins. *Archives of General Psychiatry* 29: 465–69.

COTTON, N. S. 1979. The familial incidence of alcoholism: A review. *Journal of Studies in Alcohol* 40: 89–116.

DAMON, W., AND PHELPS, E. 1989. Strategic uses of peer learning in children's education. In *Peer relationships in child development,* ed. T. J. Berndt and G. W. Ladd. New York: Wiley.

DANIELS, D. 1986. Differential experiences of siblings in the same family as predictors of adolescent sibling personality differences. *Journal of Personality and Social Psychology* 51: 339–46.

DANIELS, D., DUNN, J., FURSTENBERG, F., AND PLOMIN, R. 1985. Environmental differences within the family and adjustment differences within pairs of adolescent siblings. *Child Development* 56: 764–74.

REFERENCES

DANIELS, D., AND PLOMIN, R. 1985. Differential experiences of siblings in the same family. *Developmental Psychology* 21: 747–60.

DARWIN, C. 1892. *The autobiography of Charles Darwin and selected letters,* ed. F. Darwin. London: Dover.

DARWIN, C. 1958. *The autobiography of Charles Darwin 1809–1882,* ed. N. Barlow. London: Collins.

DE BEAUVOIR, S. 1963. *Memoirs of a dutiful daughter.* Translated by James Kirkup. Harmondsworth: Penguin Books.

DE BEAUVOIR, S. 1977. *All said and done.* Translated by P. O'Brien. Harmondsworth: Penguin Books.

DeFRIES, J. C., JOHNSON, R. C., KUSE, A. R., McCLEARN, G. E., POLOVINA, J., VANDENBERG, S. G., AND WILSON, J. R. 1979. Familial resemblance for specific cognitive abilities. *Behavior Genetics* 9: 23–43.

DeFRIES, J. C., VANDENBERG, S. G., AND McCLEARN, G. E. 1976. The genetics of specific cognitive abilities. *Annual Review of Genetics* 10: 179–207.

DIAMOND, S. 1957. *Personality and temperament.* New York: Harper.

DIXON, L. K., AND JOHNSON, R. C. 1980. *The roots of individuality: A survey of human behavior genetics.* Monterey, CA: Brooks/Cole.

DOISE, W., AND MUGNY, G. 1984. *The social development of the intellect.* Oxford: Pergamon Press.

DUNN, J. 1985. *Sisters and brothers.* Cambridge: Harvard University Press.

DUNN, J. 1988. *The beginnings of social understanding.* Cambridge: Harvard University Press.

DUNN, J., AND KENDRICK, C. 1982. *Siblings: Love, envy and understanding.* Cambridge: Harvard University Press.

DUNN, J., AND MUNN, P. 1985. Becoming a family member: Family conflict and the development of social understanding. *Child Development* 56: 480–92.

DUNN, J., AND PLOMIN, R. 1986. Determinants of maternal behavior toward three-year-old siblings. *British Journal of Developmental Psychology* 4: 127–37.

DUNN, J., PLOMIN, R., AND DANIELS, D. 1986. Consistency and change in mothers' behavior to two-year-old siblings. *Child Development* 57: 348–56.

DUNN, J., PLOMIN, R., AND NETTLES, M. 1985. Consistency of mothers' behavior towards infant siblings. *Developmental Psychology* 21: 1188–95.

REFERENCES

DUNN, J., AND SHATZ, M. 1989. Becoming a conversationalist despite (or because of) having an elder sibling. *Child Development* 60: 399–410.

DUNN, J., AND STOCKER, C. 1989. Stability and change in sibling relationships between early and middle childhood. Manuscript.

DUNN, J., STOCKER, C., AND BEARDSALL, L. 1989. Sibling differences in self-esteem. Paper presented at biennial meeting of the Society for Research in Child Development, Kansas City, April.

DUNN, J., STOCKER, C., AND PLOMIN, R. in press. Nonshared experiences within the family: Correlates of behavior problems in middle childhood. *Development and Psychopathology.*

EDEL, L. 1953. *Henry James: A biography.* Vol. 1, *The untried years.* London: Hart Davies.

EDEL, L. 1964. *The diary of Alice James.* Dodd: New York.

EDEL, L. 1987. *Henry James: A life.* London: Collins.

EDFORST-LUBS, M.-L. 1971. Allergy in 7000 twin pairs. *Acta Allergologica* 26: 249–85.

ELIOT, G. [1860] 1979. *The mill on the floss.* Harmondsworth: Penguin Books.

ELIOT, G. 1888. *Complete poems.* Introduction M. Browne. Boston: Estes & Lauriat.

ELLMANN, R. 1988. *Oscar Wilde.* New York: Random House.

ERNST, L. AND ANGST, J. 1983. *Birth order: Its influence on personality.* Berlin: Springer-Verlag.

FALCONER, D. S. 1989. *Introduction to quantitative genetics.* 3d ed. London: Longman.

FINUCCI, J. M., AND CHILDS, B. 1983. Dyslexia: Family studies. In *Genetic aspects of speech and language disorders,* ed. C. L. Ludlow and J. A. Cooper, 157–67. New York: Academic Press.

FISHER, R. A. 1918. The correlation between relatives on the supposition of Mendelian inheritance. *Transactions of the Royal Society of Edinburgh* 52: 399–433.

FORREST, D. W. 1974. *Francis Galton: The life and work of a Victorian genius.* New York: Taplinger.

FORSTER, J. 1903. *Life of Dickens.* London: Chapman and Hall.

FRIEDENTHAL, R. 1965. *Goethe: His life and times.* Cleveland and New York: World Publishing Company.

REFERENCES

FULLER, J., AND THOMPSON, W. R. 1978. *Foundations of behavior genetics.* St. Louis, MO: Mosby.

FURMAN, W., AND BUHRMESTER, D. 1985. Children's perceptions of the qualities of the sibling relationship. *Child Development* 56: 448–61.

GALTON, F. [1869] 1892. *Hereditary genius: An inquiry into its laws and consequences.* London: Macmillan.

GALTON, F. 1875. The history of twins, as a criterion of the relative powers of nature and nurture. *Fraser's Magazine,* November, 566–76.

GALTON, F. 1889. *Natural inheritance.* London: Macmillan.

GASKELL, E. [1857] 1975. *The life of Charlotte Brontë.* Harmondsworth: Penguin Books.

GERIN, W. 1967. *Charlotte Brontë: The evolution of genius.* Oxford: Oxford University Press.

GITTINGS, R. 1968. *John Keats.* London: Heinemann Educational Books.

GLACHAN, M., AND LIGHT, P. 1982. Peer interaction and learning: Can two wrongs make a right? In *Social cognition: Studies in the development of understanding,* ed. G. Butterworth and P. Light. Brighton: Harvester Press.

GLEICK, J. 1987. *Chaos: Making a new science.* New York: Viking.

GLENDINNING, V. 1981. *Edith Sitwell: A unicorn among lions.* London: Weidenfeld and Nicholson.

GOTTESMAN, I. I., CAREY, G., AND HANSON, D. R. 1983. Pearls and perils in epigenetic psychopathology. In *Childhood psychopathology and development,* ed. S. B. Guze, E. J. Earls, and J. E. Barrett, 287–300. New York: Raven Press.

GOTTESMAN, I. I., AND SHIELDS, J. 1982. *Schizophrenia: The epigenetic puzzle.* Cambridge: Cambridge University Press.

GUILFORD, J. P., AND FRUCHTER, B. 1973. *Fundamental statistics in psychology and education.* New York: McGraw-Hill.

HAIGHT, G. S. 1968. *George Eliot: A biography.* Oxford: Oxford University Press.

HAMILTON, N. 1978. *The brothers Mann: The lives of Heinrich and Thomas Mann.* New Haven: Yale University Press.

HAMILTON, N. 1983. A case of literary fratricide: The bruderzwist between Heinrich and Thomas Mann. In *Blood brothers: Siblings as writers,* ed. N. Keill. New York: International Universities Press.

REFERENCES

HESTON, L. L., AND MASTRI, A. R. 1977. The genetics of Alzheimer's disease: Associations with hematologic malignancy and Down's syndrome. *Archives of General Psychiatry* 34: 976–81.

HETHERINGTON, E. M., LERNER, R. M., AND PERLMUTTER, M. 1988. *Child development in life-span perspective.* Hillsdale, NJ: Erlbaum.

HIBBERT, C. 1967. *The making of Charles Dickens.* London: Longmans, Green, and Co.

HINDE, R. A. 1979. *Towards understanding relationships.* New York: Academic Press.

HOFFMAN, L. 1981. *Foundations of family therapy.* New York: Basic Books.

HOGG, T. J. [1858] 1933. *The life of Percy Bysshe Shelley.* Vol. 1. ed. Humbert Wolfe; quoted in Holmes (1976).

HOLM, N. V., HAUGE, M., AND JENSEN, O. M. 1982. Studies of cancer aetiology in a complete twin population: Breast cancer, colorectal cancer and leukaemia. *Cancer Surveys* 1: 17–32.

HOLMES, R. 1976. *Shelley: The pursuit.* London: Quarter Books.

HOLMES, T. H., AND RAHE, R. H. 1967. The Social Readjustment Rating Scale. *Journal of Psychosomatic Research* 11: 213–18.

HOUSMAN, L. 1969. *My brother A. E. Housman.* New York: Kennikal Press.

JACOB, F. 1988. *The statue within: An autobiography.* New York: Basic Books.

JAMES, H. 1913. *A small boy and others.* New York: Charles Scribner's Sons.

JAMES, H. 1914. *Notes of a son and brother.* New York: Charles Scribner's Sons.

JENSEN, A. R. 1969. How much can we boost IQ and scholastic achievement? *Harvard Educational Review* 39: 1–123.

JENSEN, A. R. 1980. *Bias in mental testing.* New York: Free Press.

JOHNSON, C. A., AHERN, F. M., AND JOHNSON, R. C. 1976. Level of functioning of siblings and parents of probands of varying degrees of retardation. *Behavior Genetics* 6: 473–77.

JOHNSON, R. C., McCLEARN, G. E., YUEN, S., NAGOSHI, C. T., AHERN, F. M., AND COLE, R. E. 1985. Galton's data a century later. *American Psychologist* 40: 875–92.

JOYCE, S. 1958. *My brother's keeper: James Joyce's early years.* ed. R. Ellmann. New York: Viking Press.

KAPLAN, F. 1988. *Dickens.* New York: Morrow.

196

REFERENCES

KEATS, J. 1935. *The letters of John Keats.* ed. M. B. Forman. Oxford: Oxford University Press.

KENDLER, K. S., AND ROBINETTE, C. D. 1983. Schizophrenia in the National Academy of Sciences–National Research Council Twin Registry: A 16-year update. *American Journal of Psychiatry* 140: 1551–63.

KENDRICK, C., AND DUNN, J. 1982. Protest or pleasure? The response of firstborn children to interactions between their mothers and infant siblings. *Journal of Child Psychology and Psychiatry* 23: 117–29.

KIMBALL, J. 1983. James and Stanislaus Joyce: A Jungian speculation. In *Blood brothers: Siblings as writers,* ed. N. Kiell. New York: International Universities Press.

KOCH, H. L. 1960. The relation of certain formal attributes of siblings to attitudes held toward each other and toward their parents. *Monographs of the Society for Research in Child Development.* Vol. 25, No. 4. Chicago: University of Chicago Press.

KOHN, A. 1989. *Fortune or failure: Missed opportunities and chance discoveries in science.* London: Basil Blackwell.

LAWRENCE, D. H. [1913] 1981. *Sons and lovers.* Harmondsworth: Penguin Books.

LODGE, D. 1979. *Changing places.* New York: Penguin Books.

LODGE, D. 1984. *Small world.* New York: Macmillan.

LODGE, D. 1989. *Nice work.* New York: Macmillan.

LOEHLIN, J. C., AND NICHOLS, R. C. 1976. *Heredity, environment, and personality: A study of 850 sets of twins.* Austin: University of Texas Press.

LOEHLIN, J. C., WILLERMAN, L., AND HORN, J. M. 1988. Human behavior genetics. *Annual Review of Psychology* 39: 101–33.

LYKKEN, D. 1982. Research with twins: The concept of emergenesis. *Psychophysiology* 19: 361–73.

MAAS, H., ed. 1971. *The letters of A. E. Housman.* London: Rupert Hart Davis.

MACCOBY, E. E., AND MARTIN, J. A. 1983. Socialization in the context of the family: Parent-child interaction. In *Handbook of child psychology.* 4th ed. Vol. 4, *Socialization, personality, and social development,* ed. P. H. Mussen, 1–101. New York: Wiley.

MANN, T. 1918. *Betrachtungen eines politischen.* Frankfurt A/M: S. Fischer.

REFERENCES

MANSFIELD, K. [1927] 1954. *Journal of Katherine Mansfield.* ed. J. M. Murry. London: Constable.

MANSFIELD, K. 1928. *The letters of Katherine Mansfield.* Vol. 2. London: Constable.

McCARTNEY, K., HARRIS, M. J., AND BERNIERI, F. 1990. Growing up and growing apart: A developmental meta-analysis of twin studies. *Psychological Bulletin,* 107: 226–37.

McGUFFIN, P., AND KATZ, R. 1986. Nature, nurture and affective disorder. In *The biology of affective disorders,* ed. J. F. W. Deakin, 26–52. London: Gaskell Press.

MEDNICK, S. A., GABRIELLI, W. F., JR., AND HUTCHINGS, B. 1984. Genetic influences in criminal convictions: Evidence from an adoption cohort. *Science* 224: 891–94.

MEDNICK, S. A., MOFFITT, T. E., AND STACK, S. 1987. *The causes of crime: New biological approaches.* New York: Cambridge University Press.

MENDEL, G. J. 1866. Versuche Ueber Pflanzenhybriden. *Verhandlungen des Naturforschunden Vereines in Bruenn* 4: 3–47.

MEYERS, J. 1978. *Katherine Mansfield.* London: Hamish Hamilton.

MINUCHIN, P. 1985. Families and individual development: Provocations from the field of family therapy. *Child Development* 56: 289–302.

MOSS, C. 1988. *Elephant memories.* New York: Morrow.

MUNN, P., AND DUNN, J. 1989. Temperament and the developing relationship between young siblings. *International Journal of Behavioral Development, 12,* 433–51.

NABOKOV, V. [1947] 1989. *Speak, memory: An autobiography revisited.* New York: Random House.

NATHAN, M., AND GUTTMAN, R. 1984. Similarities in test scores and profiles of kibbutz twins and singletons. *Acta Geneticae Medicae et Gemellologiae* 33: 213–18.

NEHLS, E. 1957. *D. H. Lawrence: A composite biography.* Vol. 1. Madison: University of Wisconsin Press.

NEIDERHISER, J., AND PLOMIN, R. 1990. *The importance of non-shared environment for mice as well as humans.* Manuscript.

NICHOLS, P. L. 1984. Familial mental retardation. *Behavior Genetics* 14: 161–70.

NICHOLS, R. C., AND BILBRO, W. C. 1966. The diagnosis of twin zygosity. *Acta Genetica et Statistica Medica* 16: 265–75.

REFERENCES

NUSSBAUM, M. C. 1986. *The fragility of goodness.* Cambridge: Cambridge University Press.

PAINTER, G. D. 1959. *Marcel Proust: A bibliography.* Vol. 1. London: Chatto and Windus.

PARKER, J. G. AND ASHER, S.R. 1987. Peer acceptance and later personality adjustment: Are low-accepted children "at risk?" *Psychological Bulletin,* 102: 357–89.

PATTERSON, G. R. 1982. *A social learning approach.* Vol. 3, *Coercive family process.* Eugene, OR: Castalia Publishing.

PATTERSON, G. R. 1986. The contribution of siblings to training for fighting: A microsocial analysis. In *Development of antisocial and prosocial behavior: Research, theories and issues,* ed. D. Olweus, J. Block, and M. Radke-Yarrow. New York: Academic Press.

PEDERSEN, N. L., PLOMIN, R., McCLEARN, G. E., AND FRIBERG, L. 1988. Neuroticism, extraversion, and related traits in adult twins reared apart and reared together. *Journal of Personality and Social Psychology* 55: 950–57.

PEDERSEN, N. L., McCLEARN, G. E., PLOMIN, R., NESSELROADE, J. R., BERG, S., AND DE FAIRE, U. (In press). The Swedish Adoption/Twin Study of Aging: An Update. *Acta Geneticae Medicae et Gemellologiae.*

PIAGET, J. [1932] 1965. *The moral judgment of the child.* New York: Free Press.

PIAGET, J. 1959. *The language and thought of the child.* London: Routledge and Kegan Paul.

PLOMIN, R. 1986. *Development, genetics and psychology.* Hillsdale, NJ: Erlbaum.

PLOMIN, R. 1988. The nature and nurture of cognitive abilities. In *Advances in the psychology of human intelligence.* Vol. 4, ed. R. Sternberg, 1–33. Hillsdale, NJ: Erlbaum.

PLOMIN, R. 1990. *Nature and nurture: An introduction to human behavioral genetics.* Pacific Grove, CA: Brooks/Cole.

PLOMIN, R. 1990. The role of inheritance in behavior. *Science.* 248: 183–88.

PLOMIN, R., CHIPUER, H. M., AND LOEHLIN, J. C. In press. Behavioral genetics and personality. In *Handbook of Personality Theory and Research,* ed. L. A. Pervin. New York: Guilford.

PLOMIN, R., AND DANIELS, D. 1987. Why are children in the same family so different from each other? *The Behavioral and Brain Sciences* 10: 1–16.

REFERENCES

PLOMIN, R., AND DeFRIES, J. C. 1980. Genetics and intelligence: Recent data. *Intelligence* 4: 15–24.

PLOMIN, R., DeFRIES, J. C., AND McCLEARN, G. E. 1990. *Behavioral genetics: A primer.* 2d ed. New York: W. H. Freeman.

PLOMIN, R., DeFRIES, J. C., AND FULKER, D. W. 1988. *Nature and nuture during infancy and early childhood.* New York: Cambridge University Press.

PLOMIN, R., LICHTENSTEIN, P., PEDERSEN, N., McCLEARN, G. E., AND NESSELROADE, J. R. 1990. Genetic influence on life events during the last half of the life span. *Psychology and Aging.* 5: 25–30

PLOMIN, R., AND McCLEARN, G. E. 1990. Human behavioral genetics of aging. In *Handbook of the psychology of aging,* ed. J. E. Birren and K. W. Schaie. New York: Academic Press.

PLOMIN, R., AND NESSELROADE, J. R. 1990. Behavioral genetics and personality change. *Journal of Personality,* 58:191–220.

PLOMIN, R., NITZ, K., AND ROWE, D. C. 1989. Behavioral genetics and aggressive behavior in childhood. In *Handbook of developmental psychopathology,* ed. M. Lewis and S. M. Miller. New York: Plenum.

PLOMIN, R., PEDERSEN, N. L., McCLEARN, G. E., NESSELROADE, J. R., AND BERGEMAN, C. S. 1988. EAS temperaments during the last half of the life span: Twins reared apart and twins reared together. *Psychology and Aging* 3: 43–50.

PLOMIN, R., AND RENDE, R. In press. Human behavioral genetics. *Annual Review of Psychology.*

PLOMIN, R., RENDE, R., AND RUTTER, M. In press. Quantitative genetics and developmental psychopathology. In *Rochester Symposium on Developmental Psychopathology.* Vol. 2, eds. D. Cicchetti and S. Toth. Hillsdale, NJ: Erlbaum.

PLOMIN, R., AND THOMPSON, L. 1987. Life-span developmental behavioral genetics. In *Life-span development and behavior.* Vol. 8, ed. P. B. Baltes, D. L. Featherman, and R. M. Lerner, 1–31. Hillsdale, NJ: Erlbaum.

PORTER, R., AND COLLINS, G., ed. 1982. *Temperamental differences in infants and young children: CIBA Foundation symposium 89.* London: Pitman.

QUINTON, D., AND RUTTER, M. 1988. *Parenting breakdown: The making and breaking of intergenerational links.* Aldershot, England: Gower.

REFERENCES

READ, J. 1984. Goethe and his sister: Some literary vicissitudes of a relationship. *Psychoanalytic Inquiry* 4: 573–90.

REED, E. W., AND REED, S. C. 1965. *Mental retardation: A family study.* Philadelphia: W. B. Saunders.

REICH, T., VAN EERDEWEGH, P., RICE, J., MULLANEY, J., ENDICOTT, J., AND KLERMAN, G. L. 1987. The familial transmission of primary major depressive disorder. *Journal of Psychiatric Research* 4: 613–24.

RICE, J., REICH, T., ANDREASEN, N. C., ENDICOTT, J., VAN EERDEWEGH, P., FISHMAN, R., HIRSCHFELD, R. M. A., AND KLERMAN, G. L. 1987. The familial transmission of bipolar illness. *Archives of General Psychiatry* 44: 441–47.

ROBERTS, R. M. 1989. *Serendipity: Accidental discoveries in science.* New York: Wiley.

ROOT-BERNSTEIN, R. 1989. *Discovering: Inventing and solving problems at the frontiers of scientific knowledge.* Cambridge: Harvard University Press.

ROSE, R., KOSKENVUO, M., KAPRIO, J., SARNA, S., AND LANGINVAINIO, H. 1988. Shared genes, shared experiences, and similarity of personality: Data from 14,288 adult Finnish co-twins. *Journal of Personality and Social Psychology* 54: 161–71.

ROWE, D. C. 1986. Genetic and environmental components of antisocial behavior: A study of 265 twin pairs. *Criminology* 24: 513–32.

ROWE, D. C., AND PLOMIN, R. 1981. The importance of nonshared (E_1) environmental influences in behavioral development. *Developmental Psychology* 17: 517–31.

SCARR, S. 1987. Distinctive environments depend on genotypes. *Behavioral and Brain Sciences* 10: 38–39.

SCARR, S., AND GRAJEK, S. 1982. Similarities and differences among siblings. In *Sibling relationships: Their nature and significance across the lifespan,* ed. M. E. Lamb and B. Sutton-Smith, 357–82. Hillsdale, NJ: Erlbaum.

SCHOOLER, C. 1972. Birth order effects: Not here, not now! *Psychological Bulletin,* 78: 161–75.

SELIGMAN, M. In press. *Learned Optimism.* New York: Knopf.

SHATZ, M. 1987. Bootstrapping operations in child language. In *Children's language.* Vol. 6, ed. K. E. Nelson and A. Van der Kleet, 1–21. Hillsdale, NJ: Erlbaum.

SHERMAN, M. H. 1983. Lytton and James Strachey: Biography and psycho-

REFERENCES

analysis. In *Blood brothers: Siblings as writers*, ed. N. Kiell. New York: International Universities Press.

SIMONTON, D. K. 1989. *Scientific genius: A psychology of science.* Cambridge: Cambridge University Press.

SITWELL, E. 1965. *Taken care of.* London and New York: Athenaeum.

SITWELL, O. 1944. *Left hand, right hand!* Boston: Little, Brown and Co.

SITWELL, O. 1946. *The scarlet tree.* Boston: Little, Brown and Co.

SITWELL, S. 1943. *Splendours and miseries.* London: Faber and Faber.

SMITH, C. 1974. Concordance in twins: Methods and interpretation. *American Journal of Human Genetics* 26: 454–66.

STENDHAL. 1958. *The life of Henri Brulard.* Translated by J. Stewart and B. C. J. G. Knight. London: Merlin Press.

STEVENSON, J., GRAHAM, P., FREDMAN, G., AND McLOUGHLIN, V. 1987. A twin study of genetic influences on reading and spelling ability and disability. *Journal of Child Psychology and Psychiatry* 28: 229–47.

STOCKER, C., DUNN, J., AND PLOMIN, R. 1989. Sibling relationships: Links with child temperament, maternal behavior, and family structure. *Child Development, 60,* 715–27.

SUSANNE, C. 1975. Genetic and environmental influences on morphological characteristics. *Annals of Human Biology* 2: 279–87.

TAYLOR, S. E. 1989. *Positive illusions.* New York: Basic Books.

THOITS, P. A. 1983. Dimensions of life events that influence psychological distress: An evaluation and synthesis of the literature. In *Psychosocial stress: Trends in theory and research*, ed. H. A. Kaplan, 33–103. New York: Academic Press.

TOLSTOY, L. N. [1852] 1964. *Childhood, boyhood, youth.* Translated by R. Edmonds. Harmondsworth: Penguin Books.

TOMALIN, C. 1974. *The life and death of Mary Wollstonecraft.* London: Weidenfeld and Nicolson.

TOMALIN, C. 1988. *Katherine Mansfield: A secret life.* Harmondsworth: Penguin Books.

TROLLOPE, A. [1947] 1978. *An autobiography.* Berkeley and London: University of California Press.

TROYAT, H. 1970. *Tolstoy.* London: Pelican Books.

TWAIN, M. 1966. *Autobiography.* New York: Harper and Row.

VERNON, P. E. 1979. *Intelligence; Heredity and environment.* San Francisco: W. H. Freeman.

REFERENCES

WACHS, T. D., AND GRUEN, G. 1982. *Early experience and human development.* New York: Plenum.

WATSON, J. D. 1968. *The double helix.* New York: Atheneum.

WATSON, J. D., AND TOOZE, J. 1981. *The DNA story.* San Francisco: W. H. Freeman.

WEISSBOURD, K. 1985. *Growing up in the James family.* Ann Arbor: University of Michigan Research Press.

WEST, P. 1983. Brothers under the skin: Julian and Aldous Huxley. In *Blood brothers: Siblings as writers,* ed. N. Kiell. New York: International Universities Press.

WILSON, A. 1978. *The strange ride of Rudyard Kipling.* New York: Viking Press.

WILSON, A. N. 1988. *Tolstoy.* London: Hamish Hamilton.

WILSON, J. Q., AND HERRNSTEIN, R. J. 1985. *Crime and human nature.* New York: Simon and Schuster.

WOLLSTONECRAFT, M. 1792. *A vindication of the rights of woman, with strictures on political and moral subjects.* London: J. Johnson.

WOOLF, V. 1975. *The letters of Virginia Woolf. Vol. 1 The flight of the mind, 1888–1912,* ed. N. Nicolson. London: The Hogarth Press.

YAMOLINSKY, A. 1974. *Letters of Anton Chekov.* London: Jonathan Cape.

Index

Adjustment, 81, 186
Adoption studies, 31ff, 180
Affective disorders, 16, 18f, 27, 37, 51, 81, 83, 84, 109, 140, 153, 178
Ahern, Frank M., 178, 191, 196
Alcohol abuse, 18f, 37, 51, 178
Aldous, Joan, 87, 186, 191
All Said and Done (de Beauvoir), 135, 172
Allergies, 11f, 35, 181
Alzheimer's disease, 15, 178
Anderson, S. L., 184, 187f, 191
Andreasen, N. C., 201
Angst, J., 186, 194
Animal research, 53f
Antisocial behavior, 81
Anxiousness, 16, 81
Aristotle, 137
Asher, S. R., 188, 199
Asthma, 11f, 35, 181
Attitudes, 16, 19, 49
Auditory acuity, 13
Austen, Jane, 4
Autobiography, 4, 174

Bach, Johann Sebastian, 2
Baker, Laura A., 184, 186, 187, 191
Baltes, Paul B., 129, 188, 191
Bateson, William, 146, 189
Beardsall, Lynn, 186, 188f, 191, 194

Beckson, K. 191
Behavioral traits, 12
Bell, Quentin, 140, 175, 189, 191
Bem, Daryl J., 128, 188, 192
Berg, S., 199
Bergeman, Cindy S., 200
Bernard, Jessie, 89, 186, 191
Berndt, Thomas J., 188, 192
Bernieri, F., 182, 198
Between-family environmental influence, 181
Bilbro, W. C., 199
Biography, 174
Biological determinism, xiii
Bipolar manic-depression. *See* Affective disorders
Birth order, 85, 90, 93, 186
Blending inheritance, 22
Bouchard, Thomas J., Jr., 178, 181, 192
Breast cancer, 10, 12, 35
Brontë, Branwell, 6
Brontë, Charlotte, 6, 7
Brontë, Maria, 6, 7
Brook, D. W., 188, 192
Brook, J. S., 192
Buhrmester, D., 187, 195
Buss, A. H., 173, 192

Callow, Phillip, 175, 183, 192
Cancers, 35ff

205

Cannon, Walter B., 192
Carey, G., 178, 195
Carroll, Lewis. *See* Dodgson, Charles
Caspi, Avshalom, 128, 188, 192
Chance, 135ff, 189
Chaos theory, 137f, 148f, 189
Chaucer, Geoffrey, 136
Chekhov, Anton, 192
Childs, B., 178, 194
Chipuer, Heather M., 179, 189, 200
Chromosomes, 29
Clark, A., 175, 192
Closeness, 103f
Cognitive abilities, 8
Cognitive development, 94, 157
Cohen, Donald J., 192
Cohen, P., 188, 192
Cohorts, 125
Cole, R. E., 196
Collins, G., 173, 200
Colon cancer, 10, 12, 35
Concordance, 177
Conformity, 16
Contro, 92ff
Correlation coefficient, 9ff, 28, 175f
Cotton, N. S., 178, 192
Criminality, 18f, 37, 51, 178, 182
Cumulative continuity, 128ff
Cystic fibrosis, 27

Damon, William, 187, 192
Daniels, Denise, 181ff, 186ff, 191ff, 200
Darwin, Charles, x, 22, 138, 173, 189, 193
David Copperfield (Dickens), 115
de Beauvoir, Simone, 135, 154, 172, 189f, 193
de Beauvoir, Pouqette 154
De Faire, U., 199
DeFries, John C., 178f, 181f, 184, 190, 193, 200
Delinquency. *See* Juvenile delinquency
Depression. *See* Affective disorders
Deviance, 17ff, 188
Diabetes, 10, 12, 35, 181
Diamond, Solomon, xi, 173, 193
Dibble, E., 192

Dickens, Charles, 80, 115, 185
Diet differences, 47
Disease, 8ff, 35, 47f, 177, 180f
Dixon, L. K., 179, 193
Dodgson, Charles, 7, 175
Doise, Willem, 187, 193
Dominance, 92ff
Duchenne muscular dystrophy, 27
Dunn, Judy, 173, 183ff, 187f, 189, 191ff, 197f, 202
Dyadic relationships, 186

Eczema, 11f, 35, 181
Edel, Leon, 2, 74, 93, 129, 174, 184ff, 194
Edforst-Lubs, 181, 194
Elder, Glen H., 128, 188, 192
Elephants, 182
Eliot, George, 7, 90f, 95, 112, 115f, 175, 186, 194
Eliot, Isaac, 90ff
Ellman, R., 175, 194
Endicott, J., 201
Environment, defined, 38
Environmental epistasis, 145ff
Epistasis, 29, 146, 189
Ernst, L., 186, 194
Error of measurement, 182
Extraversion, 16, 19, 37
Eyesight, 13

Falconer, D. S., 179, 194
Family systems theory, 163ff, 190
Finucci, J. M., 178, 194
Firstborn children, 68ff, 176
Fisher, Ronald, 179, 194
Fishman, R., 201
Forrest, D. W., 194
Forster, J., 185, 194
Fredman, G., 202
Freud, Sigmund, 4., 137
Friberg, L., 199
Friedenthal, R., 187, 195
Friendships, 124
Fruchter, B., 177, 195

INDEX

Fulker, David W., 184, 200
Fuller, J., 179, 195
Furman, Wyndol, 187, 195
Furstenberg, Frank, 192

Gabrielli, W. F., Jr., 198
Galton, Sir Francis, x, 8f, 12f, 26, 30, 135f, 173, 175, 178, 189, 195
Gaskell, Elizabeth, 175, 195
Genetics, x, xi, xii, 21ff, 102ff, 180f
Gerin, Winifred, 175, 195
Gittings, Robert, 5, 174, 195
Glachan, M., 187, 195
Gleick, J., 189, 195
Glendinning, Victoria, 61, 183, 195
Goethe, Cornelia, 116
Goethe, Johann W., 116, 187
Gordon, A. S., 192
Gottesman, Irving I., 178, 182, 195
Graham, Phillip, 202
Grajek, S., 178, 201
Grawe, J. M., 192
Great Expectations (Dickens), 80
Group differences, xi
Gruen, G., 181, 203
Guilford, J. P., 177, 195
Guttman, R., 182, 198

Haight, Gordon, 175, 186, 195
Hamilton, Nigel, 6, 175, 195f
Hanson, D. R., 178, 195
Harris, M. J., 182, 198
Hauge, M., 180, 196
Heart disease, 10, 12, 181
Height, 8ff, 26, 34f, 44ff, 175, 180
Heredity. *See* Genetics
Heritability, 32f. 45, 179f
Herrnstein, Richard J., 1788, 203
Heston, L. L., 178, 196
Hetherington, E. M., 188, 196
Hibbert, C., 185, 196
Hinde, Robert A., 186, 196
Hirschfeld, R. M. A., 201
Hoffman, Lynn, 190, 196
Hogg, T. J., 174, 196

Holm, N. V., 180, 196
Holmes, Richard, 174, 196
Holmes, T. H., 189, 196
Horn, John M., 178, 197
Housman, Alfred, 3, 174
Housman, Laurence, 3, 92, 174, 186, 196
Huntington's chorea, 27
Hutchings, B., 198
Huxley, Aldous, 21
Huxley, Juliette, 21, 178
Hypertension, 10, 12, 35, 181

Implications, 151ff
Impulsiveness, 16
Inbred strains, 54, 182
Interviews, 75, 185
IQ, 14, 19, 36f, 51f, 158, 178, 181, 182, 189
Irritability, 16

Jacob, François, 138, 189, 196
James, Alice, 2
James, Henry, 2, 74f, 139, 185, 196
James, William, 2
Jealousy, 63
Jensen, Arthur, xi, 173, 190, 196
Jensen, O. M., 180, 196
Johnson, C. A., 178, 196
Johnson, R. C., 175, 178f, 191, 193, 196
Joyce, James, 156, 178
Joyce, Stanislaus, 94, 96, 186, 197
Juvenile delinquency, 17ff, 37, 51, 81, 178, 182

Kant, Immannel, 137
Kaplan, F., 185, 197
Kaprio, J., 201
Katz, R., 178, 198
Keats, Fanny, 5
Keats, John, 5, 174, 186, 197
Kendler, K. S., 181, 197
Kendrick, Carol, 173, 183ff, 190, 193, 197

INDEX

Kimball, J., 197
Kipling, Rudyard, 7, 116, 139, 175, 189
Klaus, E., 186, 191
Klein, D. M., 186, 191
Klerman, G. L., 201
Koch, Helen, 62, 155, 183, 197
Kohn, A., 189, 197
Koskenvuo, M., 201
Kuse, A. R., 193

Ladd, Gary W., 188, 192
Langinvainio, H., 201
Lawrence, D. H., 7, 33, 175, 183, 197
Lawrence, Ernest, 33
Lawrence, George, 33
Learned helplessness, 144, 189
Lerner, R. M., 188, 196
Liability correlation, 177
Lichtenstein, P., 200
Life events, 17, 133, 141, 143ff, 189
Life-style differences, 47
Life-span development, 126ff, 130ff, 182, 188
Light, Paul, 187, 195
Linkage analysis, 27
Lipsitt, Lewis P., 188, 191
Liveliness, 16
Lodge, David, ix, 173, 197
Loehlin, John C., 178f, 181, 189, 197, 200
Lykken, David, 147, 189, 197

Maas, Henry, 3, 174, 197
Maccoby, Eleanor E., 181, 197
Manic-depression. See Affective disorders
Mann, Heinrich, 6, 175
Mann, Thomas, 6, 175, 198
Mansfield, Katherine, 7, 33, 60, 175, 183, 198
Martin, J. A., 181, 197
Masculinity-femininity, 16, 49
Mastri, A. R., 178, 196
McCartney, Kathleen, 182, 198
McClearn, Gerald E., 178f, 181f, 188, 191, 193, 196, 199f

McGue, M., 178, 181, 192
McGuffin, Peter, 178, 198
McLoughlin, V., 202
Mednick, S. A., 178, 198
Memory, 14, 19, 37, 52
Mendel, George J., 22ff, 179, 198
Mental illness, 8
Mental retardation, 15, 178
Meyers, J., 198
Mill on the Floss, The (Eliot), 90
Minuchin, Patricia, 190, 198
Moffitt, T. E., 178, 198
Molecular genetics, 178f
Moodiness, 16
Moss, Cynthia, 198
Mouse research, 54
Mugny, G., 187, 193
Mullaney, J., 201
Munn, Penny, 184, 187, 190, 193, 198

Nabokov, Sergei, 154
Nabokov, Vladimir, 154, 189, 198
Nagoshi, C. T., 196
Nathan, M., 182, 198
Nature and nurture, 30ff
Nehls, E., 175, 198
Neiderhiser, J., 182, 198
Nesselroade, John R., 199f
Nettles, Margaret, 185, 194
Neuroticism, 16, 19, 37
Nichols, P. L., 178, 199
Nichols, R. C., 181, 197, 199
Nitz, K., 182, 200
Nomura, C., 188, 192
Nonadditive genetic effects, 29f, 179, 189
Nonshared environment, 43ff, 130ff, 181f; in animals, 53ff
Normal distribution, 26
Nussbaum, M. C., 189, 199

Observational data, 105ff
Optimism, 144
Origin of Species (Darwin), x
Outcome links, 80ff, 108ff, 185f

INDEX

Painter, George G., 175, 199
Parental differentiation, 41, 57, 60ff, 82ff, 153, 161, 167ff, 184ff, 190
Parental influences, 60ff, 185
Parent interviews, 104
Parker, J. G., 188, 199
Partiality, 61, 167, 183, 186
Patterson, Gerald R., 157, 189, 199
Pearson, Karl, 9, 28, 175
Pedersen, Nancy L., 188, 199f
Peers, 118ff, 188
Perceptions, 154f, 162
Perlmutter, Marian, 188, 196
Personality, 8, 15, 19, 37, 48f, 178f
Phelps, E., 187, 192
Phi coefficient, 11, 177
Physical aggression, 106, 109, 157
Physical traits, 8ff, 177, 180
Piaget, Jean, 187, 199
Plato, 137
Plomin, Robert, 173, 178ff, 184ff, 192ff, 198ff, 201f
Political beliefs, 49
Pollin, W., 192
Polovina, J., 193
Polycystic kidney disease, 27
Porter, Ruth, 173, 200
Proust, Marcel, 6, 175
Proust, Robert, 6
Psychological traits, 12ff, 37, 178, 181

Quinton, David, 188, 201

Rahe, R. H., 189, 196
Reaction time, 13
Read, J., 187, 201
Reading disability, 15, 178
Rectal cancer, 11f, 35
Reed, E. W., 201
Reed, S. C., 201
Reese, H. W., 191
Reich, T., 178, 201
Religiosity, 16
Rende, R., 179, 200
Rice, J., 178, 201
Roberts, R. M., 189, 201

Robinette, C. D., 181, 197
Root-Bernstein, R., 189, 201
Rose, Richard, 188, 201
Rowe, David C., 181f, 200f
Rutter, Michael, 126, 179, 188, 200f

Sarna, S., 201
"Scapegoats," 165
Scarr, Sandra, 18, 77, 178, 201
Schizophrenia, 16, 19, 37, 49f, 178, 182
School achievement, 14, 19, 37, 52, 178
Schooler, C., 186, 201
Secondborn children, 71
Self-esteem, 83, 94ff, 153, 186
Seligman, Martin, 189, 201
Serendipity, 136
Shakespeare, William, 136
Shared environment, 43ff
Shatz, M., 184, 190, 194, 202
Shelley, Elizabeth, 5
Shelley, Hellen, 5
Shelley, Percy Bysshe, 5, 174
Sherman, M. H., 202
Shields, J., 178, 182, 195
Sibling influences, 88ff, 187
Sibling Inventory of Differential Experience (SIDE), 64ff, 97ff, 119ff, 183, 188
Simonton, Dean K., 148, 189, 202
Single-gene characteristics, 27
Singleton children, 170f
Sitwell, Edith, 61, 183, 202
Sitwell, Osbert, 61, 202
Sitwell, Sacheverell, 61, 202
Smith, C., 177, 202
Smoking differences, 47
Sociability, 16
Social comparison, 95f, 109ff, 187
Spatial ability, 14, 19, 37
Stack, S., 178, 198
Stendhal, 183, 202
Stevenson, James, 178, 202
Stocker, Claire, 184, 186ff, 194, 202
Strength of squeeze, 13
Susanne, C., 180, 202
Svevo, Italo, 21
Swedish Adoption/Twin Study of Aging (SATSA), 130ff

INDEX

Taylor, Shelly E., 189, 202
Temperament, ix, xi
Thoits, P. A., 189, 202
Thompson, Lee, 188, 200
Thompson, W. R., 179, 195
To the Lighthouse (Woolf), 155
Tolstoy, Dmitry, 6
Tolstoy, Leo, 6, 175, 186, 202
Tolstoy, Nicholas, 6, 175
Tolstoy, Sergey, 6
Tomalin, Claire, 62, 183, 202
Tooze, J., 179, 203
Traditionalism, 16
Transition points, 128ff, 188
Trollope, Anthony, 93, 186, 202
Troyat, Henri, 175, 186, 203
Twain, Mark, 1, 7, 203
Twin studies, 31ff, 180

Ulcers, 10–12, 35
Ulysses (Joyce), 94
Unipolar depression. *See* Affective disorders

Vandenberg, Steven G., 178, 191, 193
Van Eerdewegh, P., 201

Variance, 176f
Verbal ability, 14, 19, 37, 52
Vernon, P. E., 181, 203
Vocabulary. *See* Verbal ability

Wachs, T. D., 181, 203
Walpole, Horace, 136
Watson, Jon D., 179, 203
Weight, 9ff, 34f, 44ff, 175, 180
Weight difference, 10
Weissbourd, K., 203
West, P., 178, 203
Whiteman, M., 192
Wilde, Oscar, 7, 175
Willerman, Lee, 178, 197
Wilson, Angus, 175, 189, 203
Wilson, A. N., 186, 203
Wilson, J. R., 191
Wilson, J. Q., 178, 203
Wollstonecraft, Mary, 62, 183, 203
Woolf, Vanessa, 7
Woolf, Virginia, 7, 140, 175, 189, 203

Yamolinsky, A., 186
Yuen, S., 196